Stupid
about Men

Stupid
about Men

10 RULES FOR
GETTING
ROMANCE RIGHT

Deborah Dunn

HOWARD BOOKS
A DIVISION OF SIMON & SCHUSTER

New York   London   Toronto   Sydney

Our purpose at Howard Books is to:
- *Increase faith* in the hearts of growing Christians
- *Inspire holiness* in the lives of believers
- *Instill hope* in the hearts of struggling people everywhere

Because He's coming again!

Published by Howard Books, a division of Simon & Schuster, Inc.
1230 Avenue of the Americas, New York, NY 10020
www.howardpublishing.com

Stupid about Men: 10 Rules for Getting Romance Right © 2009 Deborah Dunn

All of the case studies cited in this book are composites based on notes of
actual counseling sessions conducted by the author over many years of
providing individual and marriage counseling services. However, all names are
fictitious, and important details have been changed to protect client
confidentiality. No case study cited here replicates any real client of the author.

Library of Congress Control Number: 2008048593

ISBN-13: 978-1-4165-8938-9
ISBN-10:   1-4165-8938-4

10 8 6 4 2 1 3 5 7 9

HOWARD and colophon are registered trademarks of
Simon & Schuster, Inc.

Manufactured in the United States of America

For information regarding special discounts for bulk purchases,
please contact: Simon & Schuster Special Sales at
1-800-456-6798 or business@simonandschuster.com.

Edited by Nicci Jordan Hubert
Cover design by Tennille Paden and Stephanie D. Walker
Interior design by Suet Y. Chong

for Rick, my rock,
and our children, Lee and Greyson

CONTENTS

PART I
The Lust for Fairy Dust

PART II
Into the Woods

PART III
Down in the Soggy, Boggy Swamp

PART IV
Into the Light

BONUS SECTION
And She Lived Happily Ever After . . .

ACKNOWLEDGMENTS

Never underestimate the power of a book, a teacher, a friend, or a prayer to change your life. I have been very fortunate to have experienced an abundance of all of these. I have been given priceless gifts of encouragement, spiritual wisdom, and insight through the years from so many sources I cannot name them all. Instead, I will take this opportunity to collectively thank the many authors, theologians, teachers, critics, mentors, and friends whose wise words—whether written or spoken—sustained and guided me in good times and bad. Each strengthened my faith and helped me become a better therapist, writer, wife, mother, and friend.

However, it would be terribly remiss of me not to specifically thank the authors of classic books like *The Cinderella Complex* and *The Peter Pan Syndrome*, as the inspiration for my expanded use of fairy tale themes can be directly attributed to their ground-breaking work. Likewise, I am grateful to the North Carolina Association of Marriage and Family Therapy, my fellow clinicians, and supervisors through the years who challenged my thinking and continually encourage my growth as a therapist.

Of course, inspiration translates into publication, these days, only as long as one has a good agent. In my case, that would be my agent extraordinaire, Tamela Hancock Murray, of Hartline Literary Agency, who led me to Howard Books and the editorial guidance and wisdom of Philis Boultinghouse and Nicci Jordan Hubert. It is an honor and privilege to be published by this house and to work with such a fine team of creative colleagues. I am already looking forward to getting sarted on the next book!

However, I would not have had the courage even to begin marketing this book proposal without the advocacy of my publicist and friend, Don Otis, whose calm, unwavering, and generous efforts on my behalf helped me to navigate through sometimes rough publishing waters.

Between writing, my private practice, and my disaster work (www.communityincrisis.org), I admit I was stretched a bit thin from time to time. I am thankful for my wonderfully supportive husband, Rick, who doesn't grumble when I order takeout yet again or tumble into bed practically comatose at 3 AM only to wake up looking like something the cat dragged in. And of course, there are our kids, Lee and Greyson, who consider it very fortunate that they are all grown up and out on their own, so they don't have to personally experience these things. That's okay—I know you love me, and that knowledge is the air I breathe. I hope I make you proud.

Then there are my parents and sisters, who graciously let me off the hook when it comes to family duties, especially when I have a book deadline, and forgive me when I get in a crunch and forget to call or send cards. I love you guys.

Of course, my girlfriends are in a category all their own, and you all know who you are. The weekend beach trips, lunches, prayers, tears, special gifts, and thoughtful kindnesses—I couldn't survive without them, or you. I thank God for you all!

Once Upon a Time...

. . . there was a girl who longed for true love. So when she finally met a cute guy who said he loved her, she hopped into his car, waved gaily to her loved ones, and drove off into the sunset with him, planning to live happily ever after.

But alas . . . it was not too long before our would-be heroine realized that her life was not exactly the enchanted dream she had imagined, nor was she quite as smart as she'd thought herself to be. In fact, to her utter chagrin, she began to realize that she might have made some really stupid mistakes, at least where love was concerned.

Every single one of us (well, maybe not Mother Teresa) have

a couple—or a million—"I've been stupid about men" stories we could tell. The problem is universal. We all long for the fairy-tale life, and because we believe that falling in love is the answer to all life's problems, we focus all our hopes, plans, and dreams on this happily-ever-after romance. Once we arrive in that state of profound (blinded) bliss, we ride off into the sunset believing with every fiber of our being that our lives are going to be wonderful—especially after we "adjust" our man a little, with the help of a bit of magic fairy dust.

In other words, we head into our new relationship with wish-upon-a-star, "magical" thinking and convince ourselves that if we want something badly enough we can make it come true. But in reality, we usually discover, sometimes too late, that the fairy-tale life is not all it is cracked up to be, and our men aren't quite the charming princes we'd expected.

God bless men; it's amazing the power they have over us, isn't it? Nothing can make us feel joy, passion, doubt, and insecurity more than a man. And when we do experience love gone wrong, the intensity of our feelings can blindside us. If we've had one too many crash-and-burn episodes, we begin to wonder if we'll find real love ever again.

To make our situation worse, no one seems able to tell us exactly what it is we are doing wrong. Or if they do, they preach at us, making us feel so bad about ourselves or so mad at them that we are incapable of listening, even when we know we should.

Instead, we keep on behaving as women who are precariously stupid about men (I'll call us SAM women), and we continue on the same path, hoping against hope to finally find love. We work harder at becoming sexier, prettier, thinner, or more successful. When that doesn't work, we settle for a man with whom we have little in common or even a man of questionable character. Then we go about trying to fix him, change him, rescue him, or mother him.

This book will help you end those patterns once and for all. It presents ten rules for getting romance right that will help you recover from the ten most common mistakes women make with men—the mistakes in our thinking and behavior that prevent us from finding and keeping a good man. No matter your age, marital status, cultural background, or religious persuasion, you will frequently find yourselves in these pages, and the rules will equip you for a better romantic life.

Each mistake is illustrated by a favorite folk tale or children's story written in the last two centuries—a story that was probably read to you as a child.

Those stories are so romantic and exciting, and so . . . dead wrong, at least when it comes to demonstrating how women in love should behave. Most of these fairy tales were originally written as "morality tales" for little girls; but they actually contain dangerous myths about romance and have the nerve to suggest that happily-ever-after is a result of acting on those myths. And it's these myths that keep women coming to my office for help over and over again. In this book, we will explore how these myths, and the magical thinking that accompanies them, might be sabotaging your happiness.

Instead of seeing these fairy-tale women as positive examples, you will learn how to avoid making the same mistakes they made.

If you choose to learn these ten rules and apply them to your life, you will finally understand what you need to do to get romance right this time around.

As we explore the truth about these mythical women, we'll learn the real dangers of the "Dark Forest," like the one Little Red Riding Hood travels through to get to Grandma's house. We'll start at the edge of the forest, where the mistakes we make with men are less perilous but still based on false perceptions and flawed understanding of the role romance plays in our lives.

As we progress and move deeper into the woods, where the path becomes a bit darker and lonelier, we will examine the sometimes confusing and frightening emotions that collude to drive us toward more serious mistakes, possibly even into the swamp, where all sorts of dangerous creatures hang out.

But, I promise, you'll come back out into the light and be better for the journey. You'll have a better grasp of why you've made stupid mistakes in the first place and knowledge of how to enter into healthier relationships in the future, without taking wrong turns, getting lost, or running off with the wrong guy. I've had more than twenty years of experience helping women end destructive relationship patterns in their lives, and I'm confident you can make those changes as well. There will be some challenges along the way, but the end result will be well worth the time and effort invested.

Look, I know that you are not really a stupid woman. There's no doubt that you're intelligent and successful in many areas of your life. Yet there is an alarming number of perfectly wonderful women these days who have everything—careers, education, good families, and bright futures—but still experience major problems with their love lives. If it's any comfort, the problem isn't entirely your fault; women are not the only ones to blame. There is a lot going on in our world that makes it very difficult for us to be smart. But ultimately, the responsibility for improving your romantic life is yours alone. So I'm proud that you are taking this step; it takes a lot of courage to admit you need help.

As you read this book, know that it comes from deep within my heart. I wouldn't have written this if I didn't believe in you and your ability to find happiness. I know that when you apply the ten rules for getting romance right, you will walk away with a greater awareness of why you made mistakes in the first place and what you need to do to change. You may not get the fairy-tale romance, but you will have a much better chance at experiencing *true* happiness in love and life. So let's begin this journey together so that you can become smart about men.

PART I

The Lust for Fairy Dust

ou will see the Prince at the ball, and he will be enchanted by your loveliness! But remember that you must come home at midnight, for that is when the spell ends. Your coach will turn back into a pumpkin, the horses will become mice again, and the coachman will turn back into a horse. You will be dressed again in rags and wearing clogs instead of these dainty little slippers! Do you understand?" said the fairy godmother. Cinderella smiled and said, "Yes, I understand."

—PARAPHRASED FROM THE
TRADITIONAL FOLK TALE CINDERELLA

CHAPTER 1

Cinderella

Taking Shortcuts to the Castle

A couple of years ago, I was in Florida for a television appearance promoting my first book. I called the hotel manager to my room to check on some things, and in the course of her visit we started talking about my work in regard to helping women make smart life decisions, particularly in their relationships.

She began to tell me her story. When she was in graduate school, she'd married a man because she was bedazzled by his sophistication, career, and lifestyle. Within two years of their marriage, he was cheating on her, abusing her emotionally, and neglecting their baby daughter. It was too late, she said, when she finally recognized that she had married the "package" instead of the real man. She even admitted she'd never truly looked inside that package, much less carefully examined its contents, before she married him.

As she talked, it became clear that she had danced into that relationship with Cinderella fantasies in her heart. Cinderella women believe that a man is the answer to all their life's problems. They are so enamored with the idea of being rescued that they don't really look closely at the man. Women with the Cinderella syndrome are looking for romance—which is fine and good—but they get all tangled up in the fancy wrappings of a man who seems to offer financial security, and they forget to look beyond the exterior. Almost every woman has some degree of Cinderella in her, but if you'll follow romance Rule 1: you'll be on your way to being smart about men.

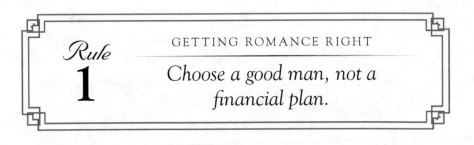

Rule
1

GETTING ROMANCE RIGHT

Choose a good man, not a financial plan.

Let's be honest. When we women think about being rescued, we usually think in terms of money. While some of us envision trips to Tahiti, a personal chef, and a housekeeper, others just want someone who will help us pay the rent on time or help us pay down our credit-card balance for a change.

Of course, even if we fantasize about being rescued, few of us marry *only* for the money. We have more going on behind our well-arched eyebrows than that. But like Cinderella, we have *issues:* dysfunctional families, personal failures, fear, boredom, loneliness, and the many obstacles we see in our paths to happiness. We crave attention and respect from a world that doesn't seem to recognize we were meant for better things . . . but we are not quite sure how we can get those better things on our own. We want short cuts to the good life, especially if we see a lot of obstacles along the way.

The subtle message we internalize (and maybe our mama even perpetuated this) is that we need to marry a lawyer, a doctor, or some other rich boy in order to get that good life. When a man comes along who fits the bill, we don't look closely enough at our motives or how we might be misleading both him and ourselves.

Heather's Story

Heather had been an excellent student, voted "Most Likely to Succeed" in her high school senior class. However, when she first came to my office, she was an exhausted divorcée raising two small boys on her own and very overwhelmed by her life.

Heather's parents had always struggled financially. Her mother was a nurse and her father was a paraplegic, injured in Vietnam when Heather was a baby. Because of this, Heather had always dreamed of becoming a doctor. However, there was little hope of affording college, much less medical school, even with the scholarships she managed to garner. That's when she met Kurt.

When Heather was eighteen, she decided to buy a used car. Kurt was the son of the car dealership's owner, had earned his degree in business, and now managed the sales force. He was quite handsome and obviously had good taste in clothes—Heather was charmed.

Although she didn't feel they had much in common, Kurt overwhelmed her with gifts, compliments, and elaborately planned romantic excursions. Heather got swept away in the glamour of it all, and before she realized what was happening, she found herself being presented to Kurt's parents.

Within months, Kurt told Heather she was the love of his life and that even though she was very young, he knew he wanted to marry her. He seemed proud of her intelligence and career goals, and offered to help her pay college expenses if she would marry him and attend day classes instead of going away to school.

Heather knew she wasn't ready to marry and that she wanted to see more of the world, but she struggled with the fear that, if she didn't marry him, she might be missing a wonderful opportunity to attain the social status she had always wanted. And marrying Kurt would allow her to stay close by and help her parents—her father's health had taken a downturn and her mother needed her. Plus, she loved Kurt . . . didn't she?

But one month after the wedding, all her college plans fizzled when she got pregnant. Heather was partially bedridden during her pregnancy, and Kurt lavished attention on her, wanting to distract her from her disappointment. Before the baby was born, he talked her into building their dream home. Heather spent her days in bed poring over house plans and ordering home goods off the shopping networks, trying not to think about her dreams of college.

A few months after the arrival of a healthy baby boy, the couple moved into their beautiful new home. But shortly thereafter, the economy took a downturn, and Kurt started spending more time at the dealership. When he finally came home in the evenings, he spent hours in his home office on the computer, following through on sales leads, while Heather spent most of her time nursing their baby and watching television alone.

Most days, Heather had the empty, quiet house to herself. Feeling very lonely and abandoned, she began to suffer bouts of rather intense depression. Unable to lose a portion of the weight she had gained with the pregnancy, she hated the way her body looked, and she felt insecure because Kurt rarely wanted to make love anymore.

But in a brief period of reconciliation, Kurt surprised Heather with a romantic "getaway" cruise. Unbeknownst to him, she went off her birth control that weekend and became pregnant again. Kurt grumbled about the expense of another baby, but since Heather once again had to spend part of the day in bed, he reasoned that the baby might be the distraction she needed. He hired a local college student as a part-time nanny for their little boy, and Heather's mom helped take care of the house.

For a while, things seemed fairly good. After the new baby was born, Kurt stayed home more in the evenings with his family. With two children to care for, Heather's life was very busy. She loved having the company of the nanny to help with the children. Her life seemed fully complete.

But Kurt began to complain even more about money. In a fit of anger one day, he let the nanny go, and suddenly Heather had to assume all responsibility for the house and children. With two very active little boys, a large house, and few interests, Heather was bored, angry, and tired most of the time. She and Kurt argued incessantly. He complained about her online shopping sprees and her spiraling weight gain, and he put her on an allowance. She accused him of using her as a maid and housekeeper, not a wife.

That is when the two, on the verge of both a divorce and bankruptcy, came into my office for marriage counseling.

Many women can relate to Heather's story. They become overwhelmed by the thought of creating a life for themselves, and just when their options seem the most limited, along comes a prince riding on that proverbial white horse (although these days it is usually a big truck, an Escalade, or a BMW!). They marry him before they are ready to be a wife, or they convince themselves that they are in love with him because he seems so able to rescue them from all their problems. All they can see is the security they think they need.

The Myth of the White Horse

One of the tools I use in therapy is asking women to write a new ending for the Cinderella story, visualizing what a girl straight from the ashes and cinders might have experienced after she moved into the castle with the prince. How would it feel to be sitting in rags by the fireplace one day, and living in a grand castle the next? Imagine the culture shock!

And when she married her prince (a perfect stranger by the way), how long did it take for her to learn to be a princess? What *did* she do? Did the royal family criticize her because she hadn't adapted to all of their snobbish ways? Did she learn that she may have had more in common with the scullery maid than with all the stuck-up lords and ladies looking down at her?

Of course, we have no clue what happened to Cinderella. We write the "happily-ever-after" ending in our imaginations. But if we read between the lines of the beloved fairy tale, it is full of surprising elements that might predict a less-than-happy outcome for the royal couple.

There are two big lies hidden in the story of Cinderella. The first is that some handsome prince is *supposed* to come along and fix things for us if we are worthy enough of him. The second is that we have to manipulate him so that he will.

The First Big Lie

Fairy tales originated centuries ago before our country was born, when women like Cinderella *couldn't* take care of themselves financially. The laws of man denied women those rights for hundreds of years. Up until the last fifty years or so, the only way a woman could ensure her financial security was to find a man with the ability to take care of her (unless she was one of the rare women who inherited wealth from her father, of course).

It took a few wars and the birth of modern technology for America to figure out that most women really weren't all that fragile or dependent, and they could take care of themselves quite well, thank you kindly. Women began to demand equal rights under the law, partly in the hopes that we would never again have to marry men we didn't love in order to have financial security.

For many women in contemporary society, this has finally become a much sought after reality. We *can* escape the poverty cycle without a man, if we work hard enough. But even so, oth-

> On some level, we still believe that it's the man's job to provide for our long-term financial security.

ers of us are still fearful, and don't trust in our own ability to take care of ourselves. No matter how far we've come, many of us have one foot back in a time when women *had* to marry in order to find a place in the world. On some level, we still believe that it's the man's job to provide for our long-term financial security.

The Second Big Lie

Because we feel unable or afraid to fend for ourselves, we somehow think we have the right to manipulate and maneuver men into marriage in order to ensure our futures. Sure, Cinderella was desperate to escape her evil stepfamily, but she did it by pretending to be someone she wasn't in order to win the heart of her prince so he could protect her. The story infers that it is socially acceptable for women to manipulate men. It encourages us to use our beauty and feminine powers to maneuver men into falling in love and marrying us before the fairy dust wears off and he sees us for who we really are.

We do subtle things to create illusions about ourselves in the minds of men, and we mislead men about who we are and what we want from life. We conveniently forget to tell our man important facts about ourselves—such as our age, bad credit score, or the number of men we've *really* had in our beds. We pretend to be smarter, more sophisticated, and more mature than we are, especially if we are very young and our prince is a good bit older than we are.

We make the mistake of not being transparent and honest about who we are until after we are married. We think our dishonesty is justified because, after all, we're just doing what we must to get our man, and all is fair in love and war.

We forget, however, that once we marry and the fairy dust begins to wear off, we are going to have to live with the consequences of those subtle falsehoods. Once the damage is done, the lie is told, or the truth exaggerated, it may take many years for relationships to heal.

Entitled to the Crown

There's no doubt that all of us have days when we want to be rescued. But one of the most significant problems we'll face—besides the consequences we'll suffer from the two big lies in Cinderella's story—comes when we allow ourselves to believe that we are *entitled* to be rescued.

Many of us are terrified to make a life for ourselves, especially the kind of life that we expect should be ours just because we are attractive or have parents who gave us everything we wanted growing up. Or maybe we didn't grow up with money or good looks, but we believe we *deserve* a financially secure future. In others words, some of us are spoiled rotten, and others of us long to be spoiled rotten. Either way, we've got problems.

> *Some of us are spoiled rotten, and others of us long to be spoiled rotten.*

But isn't that what movies and magazines tell us? Don't they lead us to believe that if we are pretty enough or know how to manipulate well enough, someone will treat us like royalty, whether it's our parents, our boyfriends, or our husbands?

Of course that is the message, and we've believed the lies hidden in that message. But whether we marry for money because we grew up without it or because we've grown up living off someone else's dime, we are compromising our future happiness and the happiness of the man we marry. Even though, like Heather, we may not realize that we have an ulterior motive, when the going gets rough, those motives begin to surface, and it is not a very pretty sight. Our so-called prince can quickly turn into a commoner, and we can begin to look a bit like a shrew ourselves.

When the Package Is Gone

So if we marry the package instead of the man, what will we do when the package is gone and there is nothing left *but* the man? (And what effects will that have on the poor heart of the man we've chosen?) Will we still be able to love and cherish him "until death do us part"? If we are honest with ourselves, probably not, especially if we feel entitled to be taken care of. It is more likely that we'd make his life miserable.

Women with Cinderella thinking are terrified of the power that money has over their lives, and that is why they want someone to rescue them from having to earn it, think about it, or manage it. It is not that these women are "gold diggers"; rather, they want someone to rescue them from having to deal with gold at all. Cinderella women would like to stay little girls but be allowed to live grown-up lives while someone else pays for it. However, staying a child financially out of fear and subsequent incapacity can make us vulnerable to men who use money to control us. This increases our phobia of money, particularly when we don't feel we have enough of it.

And fear encourages secrecy. When we are afraid, it is easy to become upset if our man questions our spending habits, or, as in Heather's case, he puts us on an allowance or tries to control us in other ways. We hide credit-card purchases, new clothing, bank overdraft notices, etc.; and ironically, we deal with our anxiety by spending more money. But no amount of purchases can satisfy us at this point. Even if we know in our hearts that spending doesn't make us happy, we still distract ourselves with planning what we can buy, whether it is a new house, a new car, or the outfit we "need" for the next big social event. Anxiety and a longing for what we think will make us less anxious start a vicious power struggle to control our hearts and minds.

What Women Really Need

It goes without saying: becoming a wife and mother is not wrong—it's a wonderful, beautiful thing for most women. And if your first priority in life is to marry and have children, then that is exactly what you should do. But there is a difference between marrying because you've found the right man and you want to live out the life you desire, and marrying as a way to *avoid* dealing with your problems, your past, or your fear of the future.

> *There is a difference between marrying because you've found the right man, and marrying as a way to avoid dealing with your problems.*

What women need is the opportunity and ability to achieve their full potential in life, with or without a man. This is not a call to avoid marriage, or to convince you that you don't need a man at all. We are meant to have companions on the journey of life, and life is not a contest to see how well you can live on your own without any help. Marriage and family are God's plan for humans. But often, if we marry without learning how to make it on our own, we cripple our ability to ever do so. We don't educate ourselves, learn how to support our children if need be, or discover our strengths as women. Then when hard times come, as they inevitably will, we are defenseless, especially if we haven't learned how to lean on God for help and comfort instead of being dependent upon our husbands.

Kurt was the object of Heather's Cinderella thinking, and he resented it, even though he was the one who initially encouraged her dependence. Heather's use of money to distract herself from her boredom and lack of fulfillment only put more pressure on him at work. When he couldn't earn enough to make her happy, his masculinity was threatened at a time when his business was going down the tubes. Of course, in therapy he finally admitted that he'd made promises in the beginning that he couldn't keep and that he had rushed her to the altar.

Heather and Kurt needed to find a place in their relationship of *interdependence* and shared power. Interdependence is simply a mutual exchange of support and a harmony in working together for common goals—exactly how healthy relationships function. Instead, Heather depended on Kurt like a child, and in return he made the mistake of treating her like one.

The fear of mastering new things is natural and simply a sign that you are on the road to learning. In an interdependent relationship it can be a wonderful joy to have someone who can support you as you follow that road.

Saying Good-bye to Cinderella

Look, if you are serious about wanting to be smart about men, and if you have believed for too long the lies the Cinderella story told, then keep the right romance rule in mind: *Choose a good man, not a financial plan.*

The most practical advice I can offer is this: grow as a person, become financially intelligent, and emotionally stronger. That means you'll have to be able to support yourself, married or not. You'll need an education and a bank account. Make it a priority to learn how to pay taxes, deal with insurance, retirement accounts, investments, and the other hard financial issues in life. The same goes for your health, dental, and car responsibilities. It's *not* smart to avoid dealing with all that by marrying.

Overall, you'll probably have to change your thinking about money and life in general. As hard as it seems, if you are in a serious relationship or even married, it's important to talk about money without overreacting and getting emotional. How do you see money and its purpose? Does it define your identity, or do you feel ashamed when you don't have any? Do you use spending money as a way to avoid having to deal with your problems?

If that is the case, perhaps money is *too* important to you. In fact, your priorities may be out of line in a lot of areas in your life, not just your financial situation. Maybe you place too much value on your beauty, the size of your house, your car, or how much you've aged. Perhaps you need to begin to define yourself by something other than numbers, other than by your bank balance, weight, age, or dress size.

Finally, continually examine your motives when you date someone. Are you more attracted to the idea of an easy life than you are to the man who offers it? Think about your childhood: how is it affecting your choices now? Do you need to face your fears, instead of looking for a way around them?

Now that you see the lies behind the Cinderella story—a fairy tale many, many women subscribe to—you have the tools needed to carefully consider your motivations, your desires, and your goals. You can choose to take positive steps toward interdependence, or you can allow the fairy dust to cloud your vision.

> *Continually examine your motives when you date someone. Are you more attracted to the idea of an easy life than you are to the man who offers it?*

You *can* build the castle of your dreams, but not when you expect someone to do all of it for you. In the long run, I promise you will enjoy the view from the window of that castle so much more when you've help build it. So take off that glass slipper, Cinderella, and put on a pair of work boots!

*S*now White took a bite of the rosy red apple, thanking the evil queen for her gift.

But the apple stuck in her throat, and unable to breathe, Snow White choked and fell to the floor, gasping for air. The queen smiled wickedly, and hurried away to her castle.

When the dwarfs returned that evening they found Snow White lying still and cold as death. Thinking she was dead, they prepared her for burial. . . . They made a glass coffin and placed it in a clearing in the forest, where they could watch over her forever. They did not know that she was not dead, but only in a very deep sleep.

One day, a handsome young prince rode through the forest. . . . He [saw] Snow White in her glass coffin. . . . Instantly, he fell in love with her. He . . . lifted the glass to kiss her. When he took her in his arms, the piece of apple dislodged from her mouth, and Snow White . . . woke from her deep sleep, and when she saw the kind, handsome prince and felt his kiss, she fell in love with him as well.

—EXCERPT FROM THE TRADITIONAL FOLKTALE
Snow White and the Seven Dwarfs

CHAPTER 2

Snow White

On Sleeping Life Away

Remember how the story of Snow White starts? A vain, insecure queen who cannot stand any female competition learns from her magic mirror that a woman in the land is more beautiful than she. Enraged, the queen plots to kill the beautiful young woman.

Meanwhile, the woman—Snow White—hides out in a cottage, which is occupied by seven dwarfs. In the Disney version of the story, she cleans and cooks for them. *Hmmmmmmmm.*

Of course, the queen finds out that Snow White is alive and feeds her the poison apple. Snow White goes to sleep. A young prince kisses her and wakes her up. They get married and live happily ever after.

At least she doesn't have to clean up after seven little weird guys anymore.

There are a lot of symbols hidden in this simple story, but one of the most implicit is that our true lives don't begin until the man of our dreams comes along. So until that blessed day, we wait, frozen, in limbo. . . .

Reasons abound for why we women find it difficult to "get a life" until a man comes along to give us one, but those reasons usually boil down to critical parents, a history of failed relationships, and emotional wounds we pretend aren't inside. Discouraged, sad, and afraid of attempting things on our own, instead of bouncing back and moving on with our lives, we "go to sleep" for awhile. We quash our dashed hopes and dreams, pretending to others that we are just fine. In the meantime, we fall into the deep trap of fantasizing about a man—a miracle man—who can kiss us, wake us up, and give us a reason to live. The shining prince will see us for who we truly are, the spell will be broken, and we will be set free from the curses of our pasts, our families, our mistakes, and our current situations.

But while we wait, many of us turn to other things to soothe our wounds and our hunger for that perfect, saving kiss—such as food, shopping, Internet relationships, or watching television. In other words, we self-medicate, and metaphorically sleep through life. See where I'm going with this, Snow White?

It is fine to want a man with whom we can share our lives, but we need to have our own lives first. After all, who was Snow White before the prince came along? Among other things, a glorified cleaning lady.

You cannot share what you don't already have. In order to do that, we must begin to understand why we're stuck where we are and learn how to get out.

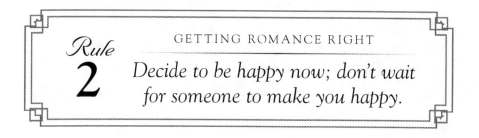

Within the image box:
GETTING ROMANCE RIGHT
Rule 2
Decide to be happy now; don't wait for someone to make you happy.

Sandy's Story

Sometimes, when we are stuck, it takes a few shocks to shake us loose, especially if we've gone to sleep waiting for someone to save us. Those shocks can bring some embarrassing truths and painful mistakes to the surface—things we would rather not face. But a shock or two could be the very thing we need to wake us up to the changes needed in order to make us happier in the long run. Sandy was a young woman in danger of sleeping through the best years of her life—until a couple of unpleasant surprises finally woke her up. A data systems analyst, she had recently been fired from her job and was having difficulty finding another.

She seemed tense and agitated during our first session and expressed anger at the world and life in general. She recounted how she felt humiliated that her dismissal had resulted from an affair with her supervisor, Jake, a married man she believed to be the love of her life.

Jake's boss learned of the affair through another employee Sandy had confided in, and he demanded that one of the two resign. Because Jake had small children to support, Sandy agreed to be the one to leave. Jake's wife also learned about the affair, so she left him. Much to Sandy's devastation, Jake did not choose a relationship with Sandy but, instead, told her that he needed to work on his marriage. Sandy was crushed at the loss of both Jake and her job, and it was days before she could even venture out of her apartment to buy food or take care of her responsibilities.

A few months later Jake called Sandy and begged to see her. He vowed that his marriage was over and that he'd be moving out just as soon as he told his children. He promised her that he would take her away—they would leave town together and get new jobs in another city.

Feeling guilty and torn, because she now considered herself to be a home wrecker, Sandy tried to say no, but found that she could not resist his arguments. Since the marriage seemed to be over anyway, and Jake had told her how unhappy he and his wife had always been, she reasoned that perhaps it was best for all of them.

Sandy refrained from calling or e-mailing Jake because he told her that his wife had hired a tough lawyer who was out "for blood," and he suspected that a PI was watching him. He claimed not to be able to know ahead of time when he could get away, so Sandy often stayed home by the phone, hoping for his calls.

Months passed and Jake continued to find reasons to stay with his wife, citing one obstacle after another, particularly with his children. Sandy began to suspect that he was not being honest with her.

Sandy began a pattern of sleeping all morning, then watching television or walking around the mall in the afternoon. She stayed up most of the night eating junk food and watching old movies. When she gained weight, she hated the way her clothes fit. She avoided job interviews because she was afraid to answer questions about why she was fired. Her credit-card balances began to spiral out of control.

Sandy finally sought counseling because of her fatigue, depression, and confusion about her relationship with Jake. As she talked, she began to realize that she may have been depressed on and off throughout her life. During her adolescence she had had frequent periods of weight gain and an unhealthy relationship with food, usually resulting from broken relationships with boys. She suffered intense struggles with a poor self-image, especially in her early teen years. Her mother, who was very thin and elegant, had constantly criticized Sandy about her weight.

She decided to end her relationship with Jake, and after much counseling, Sandy began to get her eating and spending habits under control. She started job hunting, which helped her feel much more positive about her future. She applied for jobs in other cities; and when she finally got up the courage to call the man who fired her—Jake's boss—she found that he was very willing to give her a good reference. He discreetly implied that Sandy's was not the first office affair for Jake. Of course, this was hard for her to hear, but it was information she needed to get over him once and for all. She began to move beyond a numbing depression, and a huge part of her recovery was realizing that she was choosing to build a life for herself, instead of waiting for a man to build it for her.

Positive Action

Obviously, Sandy was clinically depressed. In technical terms, depression is defined as a feeling of hopelessness, emptiness, sadness, or numbness lasting more than several weeks, which *may* be accompanied by a longing for death or perhaps a desire to "disappear" for a while. Sleeping excessively—*like a certain fairy-tale princess we know*—is a common symptom of clinical depression.

Many of us may need prescribed medication to ease the pain of our depression. Medicine is a helpful tool and a Godsend to those who need it. But if we rely on it totally, there is a good chance we won't ever get to the root of our problems. Unfortunately, many women are taking medication without doing anything positive to change their lives in the meantime. Rather than sitting around and waiting for a man to *make* us happy, we have to take *action* if we really want happiness.

Even if we aren't depressed, we can still make the mistake of putting our lives on hold while we wait for a man to come along.

Millions of apartment complexes all over the world are inhabited by women who delay building a career, investing in property, or making any significant life decisions because they are afraid if they do and a great man pops up in their life, then all their efforts would have just been a waste of time or money. They are waiting for a man to define their lives, instead of defining their own lives and inviting him to share life with them.

> *Using a husband as an excuse not to fully live is just as stupid as waiting for one to show up so we can.*

But the years go by, and they are still sitting in those apartments waiting for the prince. They are still working at the same dead-end job, still paying rent, and still waiting for the magical day they can really start living. What they should have been doing is going to school, developing skills and talents, seeing the world, and investing in their futures.

Married women do the same things, but for different reasons. They aren't waiting for the guy, but they use him as an excuse, and that is another form of Snow White behavior. Using a husband as an excuse not to fully live is just as stupid as waiting for one to show up so we can. We waste our lives when we use men and children as excuses for avoiding challenges, like getting an education, taking care of our health, reading good books, or putting aside some savings.

We too often convince ourselves that we cannot do these things unless a man helps us or that we wouldn't enjoy it alone. On the other hand, sometimes we blame the man we have for not supporting us in these risks or goals. But these are the choices we make while we eat ourselves silly, compulsively clean our houses, watch too much television, or spend all our free time shopping in the mall in order not to go crazy from boredom and the fear that life is passing us by.

Does this sound like you? It doesn't have to be this way. The cure is the same whether you are depressed, afraid, or just making excuses. Stop waiting passively for a man to give you the courage to live fully—and that means taking *positive action*.

Positive action is the opposite of passive waiting, and it involves actually setting goals (like filling out job applications, making important phone calls, etc.), taking steps to meet those goals, and following through once we have achieved those goals. Actually, the longer we delay this positive action, the more damage we do to ourselves. We run the risk of doing something really stupid to force the issue, turning to unhealthy comforts, or self-destructing in any number of lethal ways.

That is when, like Sandy, we have the greatest risk of sinking into depression and beginning the process of self-medicating. For the sake of clarity, the most common ways women self-medicate are listed and discussed briefly below. Even though these issues are hard to read and even harder to admit, it is important to own up to our behaviors when we know they apply. If we are going to take positive action beyond them, we must be aware of exactly how we self-medicate, such as by

+ Overeating

+ Overspending

+ Overworking

+ Excessive TV and Internet use

+ Infidelity

+ Thrill seeking

+ Substance abuse

Now that you've seen the list, let's look more closely at how women use each one to numb themselves to life and how you can wake yourself up.

Overeating

One of the most abused over-the-counter drugs in America is food. Women in America, particularly teenage girls, are becoming overweight at an alarming rate. It is not that we are necessarily undisciplined or that we stuff ourselves because we are out of control. Much of our overeating stems from fatigue, stress, and anxiety. We are emotional eaters. We learned early in life that carbohydrates, sugar, and dairy products had the power to comfort. When we felt lonely, sad, or afraid, we turned to a candy bar or a bowl of cereal to ease our fear and pain.

> *Food can actually set off a chemical reaction in our brains that makes us feel better—some of the same chemicals produced when a man kisses us, by the way.*

When we eat, food can actually set off a chemical reaction in our brains that makes us feel better—some of the same chemicals produced when a man kisses us, by the way. But the problem is that our pain shows up on our hips and thighs, and we end up even more miserable—unable to do the things we used to do because we develop health problems, find it difficult to exercise, and hate the way we look (especially in a bathing suit).

The answer is not in losing weight, but in getting a life. Too often we put off our lives, thinking we will do things when we lose that weight. The key is taking positive action now. When your real life starts—with or without a man!—you won't need food to comfort you so much.

Overspending

Credit-card debt is at an all-time high. One of the reasons for this is that we use shopping as a way to entertain ourselves, lift our mood, and make us feel better about our futures. Instead of living in the moment, women tend to live from one big event to the next (weddings, parties, proms, etc.). We mark time by the next date on our calendar that requires a dress or a new pair of shoes.

Sometimes this is because we are bored, other times it's because we're compensating for a lack of fulfillment within our relationships, and sometimes it's to comfort ourselves when we are between relationships. A lot of the time, it is because shopping makes us feel alive. In fact, the mall atmosphere is designed to do just that—to elevate your mood, give you energy, and excite you. After all, even if we are "asleep," we have to look good or that man we're waiting on might not want to kiss us!

We also use spending money as a form of avoidance. Instead of confronting their problems, many couples choose to go on vacations they can't afford, buy houses and cars that are way out of their budget, and generally spend, spend, spend in a compulsive effort to avoid facing the truth about their marital woes.

Debt and anxiety about finances, similar to overeating, eventually end up causing more pain in the long run. Then we run the risk of turning to even worse behaviors in our efforts to numb our emotions.

Overworking

A job is a common excuse for avoiding life. After all, we do live in America, where successful living is equated with how well you perform on your job and how much money you make. Unfortunately, this means that an addiction to work is quite socially acceptable.

That makes it easy to hide behind work, instead of facing the serious issues in our lives, like troubled marriages, financial problems, illness, or rebellious children. But doing so can badly hurt both our marriages and the quality of our parenting.

There is no doubt that making money, as well as spending it, can be a power trip. Knowing there is *something* we can do well makes us feel a lot more in control of our lives, even if everything else is going wrong, especially with those we love. We all need to feel successful, but sometimes that drive for success is the very thing that keeps from living a full and complete life.

If we fill our days with nothing but our work, we become one-dimensional people. We stop exercising or eating well, we have nothing substantive to say to our families, and we can lose important friendships, relationships, or even our marriages.

Uncorrected, even if the prince enters the picture, the future could look like this: Our children drift away from us over time and see us only for the cash we can provide. Elderly parents wait for the visits that never come, and then they are gone and it is too late. Small problems turn into huge issues, purely out of neglect.

Overwork is very unhealthy, both mentally and physically, and it's terribly boring as well. What man wants to be around a woman who can do nothing but talk about her work or who is tired and stressed out all the time? Whether that is your husband, your boyfriend, or simply someone you are dating, most good men want a woman who is fully dimensional. If you soothe yourself with work while waiting for that good man, you risk missing him altogether!

Excessive TV and Internet Use

I cannot believe the amount of time some women spend watching television or surfing the Internet! Actually, just staring mindlessly at a computer or television screen has a sedative effect on the brain, and both can be highly addictive. But what is even more addictive is convincing ourselves that the relationships we form on the Internet or with our favorite characters on reality TV are more important than the real people in our lives, or even a substitute for the relationships we don't have.

Unfortunately, I've counseled many couples whose problems stemmed from a relationship with someone they met on the Internet. They didn't necessarily go looking for a relationship— often such attachments are formed as a result of a mutual interest. It is very easy to hide behind a computer screen, using Internet romance as an escape from the drudgery of our real lives. We are still being unfaithful to our partners, even if we don't act on our feelings or ever meet in person.

Online flirtations—although thrilling and entertaining—are not exactly *quality* interactions; it is easy to present ourselves as someone we are not when we don't meet face-to-face. The truth is that you do not really know a person you meet on the Internet, and an online relationship is *not* a real relationship at all.

I could write pages here warning you about the dangers of Internet sex, pornography, and meeting men via chat rooms; but suffice it to say that this is not a healthy way to pacify yourself while waiting for the real thing to come along. And I hate to disappoint you, but soap-opera hunks go home to their real wives and children after the show is over.

Get up off that couch, girl, and get out from behind that screen. This doesn't mean that there aren't great online matching services, but sometimes sitting at the computer, instead of leading you to men, actually keeps you out of circulation.

Go out and meet some people; it's not as hard as you might think! Accept invitations to parties that you might have previously avoided because you thought you wouldn't know anyone. Ask your pastor how you can become more involved in the singles group. Get some girlfriends and make plans to meet them after work. Before you know it, you'll have so much life to live, you might stop worrying so much about men. And you know, that is exactly when a good man is the most likely to show up—when you aren't even looking for him!

Infidelity

Many people mistakenly believe that infidelity is caused mainly by the need for sex, but for women, it most often is caused by a need to feel *alive*. Just like Snow White, we want that magic kiss that wakes us up, and when our man doesn't do it for us, we are at risk for borrowing another man who will.

This subject is covered in greater depth in a later chapter, but its relevance here is specifically how women use affairs and flirtations to restore their interest in life and renew their energy, instead of doing what it takes to resolve their marital problems. Infidelity is rarely about falling in love, although we may think so at first. It has far more to do with running *away* than running *to,* and running always causes greater problems in the long run. What we run from always catches up with us.

It is absolutely true that a bad marriage can drain the life right out of us, and if we feel trapped in marriages we don't know how to fix, sometimes it feels easier to distract ourselves with another man. For a short while, the sparks fly and we are jump-started back to life once again, even if just for a short while.

But over time, infidelity steals any chance we may have of truly living a satisfying life. The only way you will truly come alive is to allow God to show you what to do about your marriage and to have the courage to be obedient when he does. In the meantime, see a good marriage counselor.

Thrill Seeking

If she is not a rock climber or a high-stakes gambler, the most common form of thrill seeking for women is getting involved with inappropriate or even dangerous partners. Whether for the high of the conquest, the thrill of the hunt, or the rush that comes from taking risks with strangers, this is seriously life-threatening behavior—and it must be stopped if a woman really wants to have a healthy life.

The purpose of thrill-seeking behavior is to flood the brain temporarily with powerful hormones designed to excite the brain, which is often depressed and numb in the absence of a high degree of outside stimulation. But the downside of this, besides the physical danger involved, is that after the thrill is over, the depression and numbness return in greater measure, thus requiring greater risks and more dangerous thrills the next time around. The behavior can quickly spiral out of control, especially when using drugs and alcohol, as is most often the case.

The most negative aspect of this is that in order to continue to enjoy the "chase," over time a woman has to shut off her conscience. She has to quit listening to her own inner voice and, in the process, forgo developing her real talents, gifts, and growth as a person. After awhile, even if the body and the brain feel more alive, the soul and spirit start to die.

Substance Abuse

Perhaps the number one way women sleep their lives away is by abusing alcohol or drugs. We all know about the problem, how it starts, and how insidiously it can destroy lives. All of us know someone, maybe even a woman we love, who uses alcohol or drugs inappropriately.

Anything that makes you high temporarily has the potential to become a long-term depressant.

Often young women start drinking alcohol or doing drugs in high school and college so they can appear sophisticated, so the guys they want to impress will think they are mature. But I've taught drug education for several years to high school students, and I've worked as a therapist for a women's rehab center nearby. And just about all of these women, including the high school students, are stupid about men. It seems that substance abuse goes hand in hand with unhealthy relationship habits. After awhile it is difficult to determine which comes first—the depression or the substance abuse.

Anything that makes you high temporarily has the potential

to become a long-term depressant. In other words, the more you use a substance to avoid depression, the greater your chances for becoming severely depressed in the long run and the bigger the mistakes you will make with men.

Waking Yourself

Isn't it amazing that Snow White never aged while she slept? Wouldn't we love to freeze time, at least every now and then, and take a long, lovely rest? Too bad we don't get that luxury.

Truth is, being fully awake also means feeling our pain and facing some hard times. But trust me, friend: the hard times we're tempted to sleep through really *do* serve to help us learn and grow and become stronger, better people. That is the whole point of life—to learn and to grow, and to be all that we can be while we have this brief space of time to share our hearts with others. Every day that we choose to waste by not fully living is a day we've lost forever. Time passes and we get older, whether we sleep through it or not.

I realize that many of you are struggling terribly with situations I don't know or understand, and I'm not trying to gloss over anyone's pain. There are plenty of women who dream of going to sleep and never waking up at all—maybe you've been there. I certainly have, but I'm thankful that I lived to see a brighter, more hopeful day.

If this mindset describes you, I hope you are getting the professional help you desperately need to deal with your situations.

I can promise you there is a brighter day waiting for you, if you just hold on long enough. If you cannot afford a private counselor, seek out a pastor, a wise friend, a mental-health center, or a nonprofit organization in your area that offers depression screening, medication assistance, and free or sliding-scale-fee counseling services.

But if you do not need medical assistance, there should be nothing stopping you from beginning to take the risk of embracing a present, joyful *life* now. The only way to really get a life is to face it head on . . . with guns blazing.

Taking Baby Steps

If you're ready to make some changes toward choosing to be happy now, I'd encourage you to take some baby steps on your journey toward coming awake. You don't have to conquer the world overnight. Plan a small vacation with girlfriends—not to drink, party, or manhunt—but to see a place you've never been before. Enroll in a community college course or sign up for a leisurely seminar, perhaps something like cooking or scrapbooking.

If you've gained weight, set a goal to lose five pounds instead of thinking about how much you really

> *Stop fantasizing about how different your life would be if the right man would come along. You are the only one with the power to change your life.*

need to lose. When you've done that, let your body adjust and then lose five more. Journal your daily struggle to overcome your fears and emotions.

But most of all, it is important to stop fantasizing about how different your life would be if the right man would come along. You—not a man, regardless what the song lyrics and the movie scripts say—are the only one with the power to change your life.

The funny thing is that if you quit looking for a man to wake you up to life and if you start making our own happiness, you'll learn you don't need him nearly as much as you thought you did. And, sure enough, that is when the right person often comes along.

It's funny how that happens, but absolutely true. It is when we aren't sleeping—when we are content with our lives, our work, and ourselves—that we attract men who want to share life with us. And when we work on our own selves, instead of blaming our husbands, our marital problems start to resolve.

This is a key concept for us to remember, and it will resurface at various times throughout this book. Men want to *share* our lives, not *provide* that life for us.

See, it comes!" cried Curley, pointing to the heavens. Wendy was almost overhead, and they could hear her plaintive cry. But more distinct came the shrill cry of Tinker Bell. The jealous fairy had now cast off all disguise of friendship and was darting at her victim from every direction, pinching savagely each time she touched her.

"Hullo, Tink," cried the wondering boys. Tink's reply rang out:

"Peter wants you to shoot the Wendy." It was not in their nature to question when Peter ordered them. "Let us do what Peter wishes" cried the simple boys. "Quick, bows and arrows!"

—J. M. Barrie, *Peter Pan: The Original Story*

Tinker Bell

Why Fairies Get Flattened

It seems astounding that a children's book writer would create a female character—a fairy—who actually tries to kill off another character. All because of a boy like Peter Pan, for goodness' sake!

But while we typically think of fairies as being helpful and sweet, in folklore, fairies are actually sinister little creatures. They lust after human men, manufacture all sorts of pranks and plots, and have very little conscience. True to fairy lore—which makes it clear that fairies are implicitly sexual beings—Tinker Bell is aggressive, jealous, and sexually provocative, even if she *is* a character in a children's story. That's why she makes such a fine example of the kind of woman this chapter will address—the SAM (stupid *about* men) woman who does whatever she must in order to get the man, including misusing her sexuality.

Nonetheless, we love Tinker Bell and all fairies like her. All you have to do is Google *fairies*, particularly *Tinker Bell*, on the Internet, and the number of sites that load is amazing. Fairies have what could be considered a cult following.

But the funniest are the "pressed fairies"—you know, the ones in a book that was published a few years ago that depicted them looking like a bug zapped flat on a windshield—spread-eagled and shell shocked. Meant to appear as if someone has captured, and then pressed them like flowers between the pages of a book for safekeeping, the expressions on their faces are priceless. They are a bit macabre, I know, but what a great metaphor for what happens to us when we are stupid about men, particularly when it comes to sex.

Like those flattened fairies, we can eventually have the life squashed out of us, especially when we are jealous of other women, sexually promiscuous, vindictive, and manipulative. In the process, we hurt ourselves, the men who love us, and other women.

Tinker Bell behavior isn't limited to blondes, no matter what some people think. Women in all shapes, sizes, colors, ages, social classes, and ethnic groups mimic Tink. Sexual misuse is becoming epidemic, and the stats on sexually transmitted disease and sexual addiction prove the point.

Not all of us habitually misuse sex and sexuality, though many of us have been guilty of it from time to time. We haven't all set out to intentionally hurt women, either, though many of us have. But to be honest, many of us have been guilty of capricious flirting and placing more emphasis on being sexy than being smart. Because it seems to be so much fun at the time, and even somewhat innocent, we buzz around with a glow in our butts, oblivious to the many flyswatters hovering, waiting to come down and squash our fast little fairy selves.

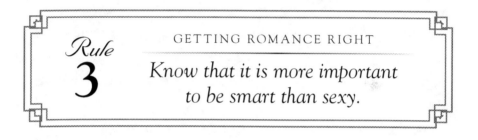

Rule
3

GETTING ROMANCE RIGHT

*Know that it is more important
to be smart than sexy.*

To understand this rule, we'll look at Tammy, a real-life Tinker Bell, and then we will examine Tinker Bell behaviors, learn where they might originate, and what to do about them.

Tammy's Story

Tammy, her hair perfectly highlighted and her nails immaculate, walked confidently into my office. Wearing a sundress that showed off her tanned and lithe figure, she was the picture of health and vitality.

But as I heard her story, I learned that she was not healthy at all—not by a long shot.

Tammy's husband, a prominent attorney in town, was threatening to file for divorce and assume custody of their children. Tammy was terrified, not only because she might lose her children (ages four and six), but because she couldn't fathom starting all over without any income, or having people think she was a bad mother.

As we talked, it became apparent that she had a long history of frequent sexual activity. Her parents had divorced when she was in her teens, and her mother celebrated her newfound freedom by partying and going out on lots of dates, sometimes with married men. Although Tammy's father had actually divorced her mother over this issue, Tammy claimed not to care much one way or the other.

Mother and daughter enjoyed hearing about each other's romances and sharing clothes and jewelry. Her mother rarely questioned her daughter's sexual experiences, except to vaguely advise her to "be careful." When Tammy was fourteen, her mom took her to a nurse practitioner for birth control and told her that whatever she did, not to get pregnant—or "sick," as she put it.

Tammy took this as implied permission to live as she wished. With little supervision, no real role model, and a gorgeous body, her sexual escapades included having sex with her sister's boyfriend and a string of one-night stands throughout the years. When she was sixteen, she got pregnant. Relieved when she miscarried a few weeks into the pregnancy, she never told anyone about it.

Her party lifestyle ended when she married, although she missed her days of flirting with anyone she pleased, and she sometimes felt as if she were "all dressed up with no place to go." Men still "came on" to her—after two children, she still had a body that most women envied, and it was difficult not to respond. But she loved her husband and explained to me that she really hadn't thought she was the kind of woman who could cheat on her husband.

All that changed when her husband's old college roommate came into town. It was a stressful time in their marriage and business, and Tammy was bored and lonely. The couple went out to dinner with the man and his wife, and in the course of the evening, Tammy drank a bit too much and started flirting openly with her husband's friend. After awhile, the wife, rather quiet and shy, asked to leave. The next day the friend called her to "apologize" for his wife's departure. The two began talking and meeting for drinks, which resulted in a very stormy and dramatic affair that lasted for a couple of years.

Tammy's lover eventually divorced his wife, but once the divorce was final, he began seeing not only Tammy but also younger women. Insanely jealous because she thought the two would marry, Tammy confronted him, and the affair abruptly ended. But in the meantime, her husband learned of the affair and immediately filed for divorce.

Tammy was able to keep custody of her children, and her husband paid enough child support so that she could maintain a comfortable lifestyle. Her old lover, however, was still dating younger women, and Tammy realized she had never loved him. Once her divorce was final, she was angry at herself for allowing the affair to cost her the marriage.

Tammy's counseling involved restructuring her values, priorities, and her casual approach to sex, married men, and her treatment of other women. It was a difficult process for her, because her sexual attitudes had been learned from a very young age. As with many SAM issues, we can usually trace our sexual mentality to our childhoods.

Sexy or Smart?

A research study recently reported that 80 percent of teen girls polled in America stated that it was more important to be considered *sexy* than *smart*. This did not surprise me, but it did make me sad. That is exactly what Tinker Bell thinks.

In spite of progress in most other areas of their lives, girls appear to have actually regressed when it comes to their views of what makes them valuable as human beings, and that is very, very serious. It is almost as if we've totally returned to the cave days, when being "valued" meant being bonked over the head with a club and dragged back to a cave. It means we've lost hundreds of years of progress in our quest for equality because we've confused sexual power with personal power.

> *In our quest for equality, we've confused sexual power with personal power.*

And just why do girls believe that their ability to seduce a man defines their value as a woman—especially at a time in history when they are finally coming into their own financially, educationally, and legally? It is directly related (but not limited) to the barrage of marketing that beats a girl on the head from the time she is born until her death.

From the day they first sit straight in their high chairs, until the day they are finally wheeled into the morgue, females of all ages are subjected to a continual stream of messages that tell them they must be sexually desirable. And sexually desirable isn't a general idea; we have been given a very specific outline for what a sexually desirable woman supposedly looks like.

This is complicated by the fact that millions of girls from age twelve to twenty now have more discretionary income than ever before in history, and the gross national product is absolutely dependent on getting them to spend it. Corporate America (followed closely by Japan) has figured out many clever tricks and mind-manipulating tactics to speed up the rate at which girls spend their money, and the primary method is to convince these girls that they must be sexy in order to be happy and that buying yet another product will make them sexier. In other words, little Tink, you've been *had*.

Do we really think about the onslaught of advertising that portrays girls bumping, grinding, and thrusting their way to what the ads suggest will bring blissful happiness?

If we did, we might cause a fuss. But instead, we seem to lap it up. We all know that sex sells, even if the product being sold doesn't have anything to do with sex. We still fall for the lie. And the cumulative effect of all this exposure to erotic suggestion is enormous—so great that the Centers for Disease Control and Prevention (www.cdc.gov) reports that almost 40 percent of all teens under the age of eighteen are now reported to be sexually active, often with disastrous consequences.

None of us are immune. We have bought into the lie that if we aren't getting a lot of sex and romance, something is wrong with us—even those happily married, celibate, or trying to stay virgins. We believe that in order to be powerful, men must want us, even when we don't particularly want them back or have any plans to initiate sex with them. Something in us believes that men are *supposed* to be attracted to us, and other women envious of us, if we are worth our salt.

But when it is all said and done, what have we really accomplished in the end? Are we happier, healthier, or more successful because we can turn a few heads and raise a few eyebrows? Ironically, statistics show that we are not.

The Lessons of Little Tink

Do you remember how it felt to be in middle school? Perhaps you were one of those girls who never hit the awkward stage. You know, one of those girls who seemed to know secrets about life others didn't—the girls who could attract boys like bees to honey.

Perhaps, on the other hand, you were one of the girls who envied them. I know I was. After all, they had what we wanted, and we thought they were having all the fun—while we sat at home on Saturday night wondering why the phone never rang. Whatever *it* was, we wanted *it*, even if we didn't have a clue how to use *it* appropriately.

Those golden girls seemed to have all the luck in other things as well. It was bad enough they didn't suffer a single pimple, an extra pound, or a care in the world. They were on autopilot, headed for happily-ever-after—complete with wonderful husbands, great careers, smart kids, and fabulous homes. They were the girls living in the Magic Kingdom.

On the other hand, we got acne, gained weight, and said the wrong things. And because we were unsure of ourselves and self-conscious, especially when we were around boys, we were silly, loud, and showed off too much. In other words, we were typical teenaged girls.

But in our hearts, we anxiously wondered why *we* hadn't been touched with the magic fairy dust. Weren't we good enough? Weren't we pretty enough? What was wrong with us?

And so it began. In our insecurity and desire to attract boys, we started playing games, competing with other girls, and doing *whatever* it took to prove we could be just as popular, just as desirable, and just as much fun. We became little Tinks—sometimes, we were even *vicious*, just like our fairy-tale counterpart.

And of course, we got burned in the process. People who play games with their lives usually do. Some lost their virginity to guys who treated them badly, others sacrificed best girlfriends over boys, and some found themselves in situations where they were sexually exploited—including even date rapes or an abortion. Because of our misconstrued concepts of how to attract men, we suffered through some tough lessons.

The fortunate among us narrowly survived with our dignity, hearts, and self-esteem intact. Thank goodness, lots of us learn from our mistakes, and many of us self-correct. We cease our sexual game playing, learn not to betray girlfriends, and finally realize that our value as women isn't determined by how many males want us. We grow up and become mature, responsible women who treat our bodies and our friends with great respect.

But that is the difference between girls who are smart and those who are dangerously stupid about men. Smart girls learn from their mistakes. SAM girls don't. They just keep on doing the same things over and over again, especially when it comes to men and sex, and as games become more vicious, the stakes get higher.

Who Are the True Tinker Bells?

As you realize by now, all of our folk-tale heroines have dark sides. Tinker Bell is no exception. Unlike the everyday flirt whose behavior is relatively harmless, Tinker Bell holds no illusions about her innocence. She may not always be overtly promiscuous (although most fairies are), but she will certainly think nothing of using every arrow in her arsenal (including sex) to get what she wants—whether it is a cute boy and popularity in high school or, later in life, the man she badly wants to be hers, even if he belongs to someone else.

There are four underlying factors that all serious Tinker Bells seem to have in common:

1. The need for constant affirmation that they are desirable

2. The need for high amounts of attention from the opposite sex

3. A tendency to define relationships solely by physical attraction

4. Sexual addiction

Tinker Bells are extraordinarily insecure and yet terribly vain. Because of this, they crave affirmation and attention, and the easiest way to get it is by arousing a man, even when having sex in and of itself is not that important. That is why they define a good relationship by how sexually charged it is—that is how they gauge their own value. They desperately need to know they have the power to make a man want them, because it is the only power they feel they have.

This can evolve into a sexual addiction over time, because sex becomes a drug that a Tink uses to avoid serious issues in life. It keeps the endorphins and dopamines rushing to her brain, makes her feel beautiful (at least in the moment), and infuses her with energy. She gets "high" off the game of sexual conquest and lives from one sexual encounter to the next.

> *Tinker Bells desperately need to know they have the power to make a man want them, because it is the only power they feel they have.*

This is not to say that Tinker Bells are totally incapable of love or romance. There is often more going on than just lust and physical attraction, although that is the primary element by which many Tinker Bell women measure the quality of the relationship.

In fact, many women are after more than just sexual conquest—much more. The ultimate "high" is getting a guy to fall in love. Many of us want to own a man's heart, even if we don't particularly need it or plan to keep it. To some, it is a challenge to keep hearts on the line, and just as soon as a guy figures this out and tries to cut bait and leave, many of us will do all sorts of manipulative things to pull him back in. It's all about power, at least at that point.

Many women with Tinker Bell tendencies don't realize that the need for this kind of power actually weakens them over the years. Besides wasting time in relationships that only fill the need for attention and distraction, this can keep them from forming solid commitments with good men and being truly intimate with them.

Sex Mates or Soul Mates?

There seems to be a lot confusion these days about the difference between sexual intimacy and emotional intimacy. We automatically assume they are one and the same. But the truth is that sexual intimacy, especially if it comes too soon in a relationship, often serves as a barrier to the deepening of emotional intimacy.

Nothing stops a relationship cold in its tracks faster than sex initiated too early. Once a relationship becomes sexual, all focus and intention turns to the quality of the sexual experience—

when to have it, where to have it, and how to have it. Communication often comes to a standstill, at least after a few months, because it is assumed that because we are having sex, we know the person. And for both men and women, anxiety sets in about the nature of the relationship and the direction in which it might be headed. Energy turns toward sorting out the true intentions or perceptions of the other and attempting to second-guess what their expectations of the relationship might be. Honest sharing often ceases, out of fear of doing or saying **anything that might "scare"** the other person off or of learning what the other person truly thinks and feels about the relationship.

> *Nothing stops a relationship cold in its tracks faster than sex initiated too early.*

Because of a chemical cocktail released during sex—made up of dopamine, norepinephrine, and PEA (which also regulate serotonin and endorphins)—we experience an immense surge of heightened well-being, peace, relaxation, and high energy. But once those chemicals are released, their magic begins to lose potency. This is when many, especially men, who are addicted to the rush of being in love and sexual conquest, will abruptly abort a relationship, with no contact, until that sexual high is desired once again.

And once each person in the couple "wakes up" and begins to realize he or she really doesn't know the person he or she is having sex with, then suddenly, the individual begins to notice all the negative things about the other person that were overlooked in the heat of romance and sexual yearning. All of a sudden, there are all sorts of things to criticize, the two may begin to avoid each other, and they eventually allow the relationship to die altogether.

But there is an added element. People who jump into bed too fast often *want* to keep others at an emotional distance. They may be emotionally immature, keeping secrets, or they may just be afraid to let another have any kind of power over them. A real Tink is notorious for using sex to keep men at an arm's length. She is afraid that someone will see into her heart, and that would make her vulnerable; and to be vulnerable means to feel powerless. Remember, Tink is all about power.

She may get married, especially when she is very young, just because it feels so grown up and makes her feel powerful. But because of her bent toward manipulation and conquest, she is not above pretending to be pregnant or stealing another woman's husband. She believes these ploys are fair and right—if she cannot get a man any other way.

Getting married and having babies may seem like fun for Tink but once a woman has what she thought she wanted, she can quickly tire of her husband and begin to resent her children for making her feel old.

She may cool her heels for awhile, but once the romance wears off and her husband fails to pay her enough attention, her eye may wander. This is when she reverts to her sexual past once again, and she ends up like Tammy, in a whole lot of emotional and marital trouble.

Serial sexual relationships with little emotional intimacy characterize much of dating these days. Sadly, it means that women who *could* have had meaningful long-term relationships with men aren't able to. Many men *are* capable of committed relationships. Despite popular opinion, a man's brain is not located in his male "anatomy," and men do not think solely about sex. But once aroused, sex *is* all they can think about—particularly with you, if you are the one who got them started.

SAM women often equate arousal with the beginning of love. They do not understand that sex does not win the heart of the man, even though at the time he may actually feel he is falling in love with the woman. He may not be lying *in the moment*. But if you succumb to his advances or throw yourself at him, trying to get him to fall for you, it will only serve to distance him emotionally. He will become anxious and fearful that you want a commitment now that you have "given it up," and this encourages him to see only what is wrong with you instead of what is right.

That is when you might get flattened, dear fairy girl, because serial sexual relationships over a period of time often decrease your ability to form intimate relationships and experience good sex with a man you really love. And in the meantime, you lose the respect of coworkers, friends, family, and the men you really would like to attract into your life.

When Fairies Get Flattened

Here are some of the more glaring statistics about the consequences of Tinker Bell behavior:

1. The average age a girl becomes sexually active is sixteen. A girl's brain and emotions are not fully developed until she is around the age of twenty-one to twenty-five. This means many female children are having sex before they are mature enough to handle it.[1]

2. A recent CDC (Centers for Disease Control and Prevention) study reports that one in four of every girl between the ages of twelve and nineteen has a sexually transmitted disease.

3. In 2007, nearly half of pregnancies among American women were unintended, and four in ten of these 22 percent were terminated by abortion. In 2005, 1.21 million abortions were performed in the United States.[2]

4. Sexual promiscuity at any age of life is statistically linked to depression, suicide, and relationship difficulties (divorce, family problems, parenting issues, etc.) throughout life. This link is more significant if abortions or sexually transmitted disease are factors. The earlier the behaviors begin, the greater the problems.

5. Depending on the source, anywhere from 30 to 50 percent of married women report they've had an extramarital affair. In its July 2004 issue, *Newsweek* reported on "the secret lives of wives," in which marriage experts noted that 30 to 40 percent of their female clients had cheated on their spouses. Others have even claimed that percentage is closer to 50 percent.[3]

6. There were approximately 13,274 divorces in 2007 in

CHAPTER 3 *Tinker Bell*

America directly attributed to extramarital affairs. (That number is based on 2,169,000 marriages from September 2006 to September 2007.) Multiple sources indicate that 40 to 60 percent of all marriages will end in divorce.[4]

7. There are 4.181 million unwed moms who have never married and another 3.392 million single moms who are divorced raising children.[5]

8. Four out of ten sexually active students report no or infrequent contraceptive use.

9. Female students having multiple partners were especially likely not to use protection.[6]

10. The number of women with AIDs in the United States in 2007: 126,961.[7]

I hope these statistics have been sobering enough that if you see yourself in Tinker Bell, you are becoming ready for change. Keep reading. It's not too late.

Getting Rid of Tink

It is hard to stop unhealthy sexual behaviors after you've become entrenched in them. Perhaps you believe being sexually promiscuous is just who you are. It's how your mother acted or the way your friends behave, so it has become normal for you. Or maybe you've become addicted to the game itself. But even if you use your sexuality as a way to compete and get attention, that doesn't mean you are overcome by excessive lust. A heightened sex drive has been related to hormonal imbalance or chemical imbalance in the brain, such as that caused by bipolar illness, pituitary gland malfunction, or other disorders.

However, it is possible you may not even like sex all that much. You might even dislike men, as strange as that may sound, especially if you were the victim of sexual abuse. You may have become what therapists call sexualized, someone who has been groomed early in life to believe that she exists to meet the sexual needs of others. If you were conditioned as a child to engage in sex with adults or other older children, you may believe that your only role in life is to deliver sexually or that your only *value* is in your sexuality.

Your sexuality is a gift, not a toy in a game or a weapon to be used against others. Gifts must be protected and valued, not given away to strangers.

You may have even decided at some point that you were damaged goods, so you might as well take advantage of your sexuality to get your way, since someone took advantage of you.

On the other hand, you may simply be substituting the ability to seduce a male for real accomplishments in life, or perhaps you are bored, lonely, insecure, or angry. Sex may just be a game for you.

If sex is a game to you, and you aren't dealing with any major issues from your childhood regarding sex, then the only way you are going to be able to change is to drop out of that game.

This doesn't mean you can never enjoy sex again, not at all. Sex is wonderful in its proper context—specifically, in marriage—and I'm certainly not asking you to give it up. I'm simply asking you to approach it more carefully. You must step back from your behavior long enough to see what you are doing and break your addiction to male attention.

Stepping back will give you a new perspective and allow you to begin treating yourself and others with respect. You will begin to see your sexuality as a gift, not a toy in a game or a weapon to be used against others. Gifts must be protected and valued, not given away to strangers. You are giving yourself away when you engage in casual sex, and you are a precious jewel, not a cheap piece of junk or a pawn in a game.

If you enjoy risk and adventure, learn to achieve that "rush" in a way that is healthier. Do something more beneficially adventuresome than having an affair, flirting, or getting a breast enhancement so you'll look sexier. Learn to fly an airplane or jump out of one. Go mountain climbing. Run marathons or scuba dive. At the very least, buy a can of paint and paint your apartment a daring color. You might discover you can do things you never dreamed would be half as exciting as they are!

It's also a good idea to work on becoming a woman whom other women can trust. As you age and your ability to attract men dwindles (and sadly, it *does* dwindle), you are going to need women you can trust in your life to support, love, and comfort you along the way.

It is important for you to learn to develop relationships with others that have nothing to do with sex. This is difficult for a

Tinker Bell, who is used to acting impulsively on her sexual prowess. But you can sustain professional relationships and friendships without acting on them sexually if you work hard at it.

But a word of warning on that note: do not fool yourself into believing you can have friendships outside of work with married men, or that if you are married yourself, you can have similar friendships with guys. That would be like putting an alcoholic in a bar and telling him or her not to drink. It would probably be good to stay away from R-rated movies and sexually explicit books for the same reason—particularly erotic romance. They just fuel the fire.

It's All in Our Minds

We are sexual beings, and our sexuality is an expression of our inners selves. Sex *is* a good thing and meant to be enjoyed with the right person, at the right time in our lives. It is meant to be part of the food of life that sustains us and deepens our connections to those we truly love.

As both a Christian and a licensed therapist, I've come to understand the wisdom of biblical teachings about abstinence until marriage. God isn't out to keep us from having a good time. He knows our sexuality is a very powerful force in our lives and, if misused, can harm us. Statistics on divorce, sexual health, emotional stability, and marriage all confirm the validity of God's plan for sex and marriage.

But I'm aware many of you are very far from this thinking in your own lives. You may already be sexually active outside of marriage, or you may have a long history of sexual relationships with many partners.

God understands and so do I. He forgives you and can help you with that, no matter who you've been with and what you've done. It may not be easy to change, but I can promise you that you will be happier in the long run. The more you try, the more strength you will find inside of yourselves to live a healthy life.

If we treat sex like fast food—cheap, hot, and quick—we end up starving for real love and connection. If we misuse our bodies and our power over men to fill the emptiness in our hearts, our spirits, and our lives, we eventually start dying on the inside, no matter how beautiful or sexy we appear on the outside. Sex has the power to sicken us if not treated as the precious life-giving gift that it is.

On the flip side, what constitutes a healthy sex life with a man? What does that look like?

A healthy sexual relationship should ideally be an extension of a mutual sharing of thoughts, feelings, and interests—a comfort to both of you that provides nurture and solace. It feels good all over—not just in your body, but in your heart and soul. You don't feel diminished, guilty, or sad once it is over. Instead, like anything else positive in your life, it will leave you feeling stronger, empowered, and recharged, rather than disappointed, anxious about the future, and somehow unclean. And those feelings will last over time—not just until you realize you are in bed with someone you don't truly love, because it felt good in the moment.

This means your partner has to be emotionally, legally, and spiritually available to you. You have to know beyond a doubt that he wants all of you—not just your body—but your heart and mind as well. He doesn't engage you in clandestine behaviors that require you to sneak around, and if he truly loves you, he will never ask you to lie.

He tells you up front if he has an STD or if he ever got someone pregnant, and you will know ahead of time how he feels about birth control, abortion, and anything having to do with sex itself. He doesn't leave all that stuff up to you and act as if it has nothing to do with him.

But the irony is, our bodies are made so that when we are physically attracted to a man, the thought of sex is so enticing that it is difficult to think clearly. The sexual hormones that surge through our brains send the blood rushing straight to our heart and our genitals. It becomes extremely difficult to think, reason, or stop ourselves from taking physical contact to the next level.

For those of us who are lonely or starved for affection, the ability to deny ourselves becomes nigh on impossible. That is why it is crucial to guard your heart and to avoid compromising situations with men. Don't set yourself up for failure and encourage inappropriate sexual contact by spending too much time alone, whether with a new acquaintance, a coworker, or a married male friend. The temptation is just too great, and once you step over the line, it is very difficult to rein your feelings back in.

This Little Light of Mine, I'm Gonna Let It Shine

Okay, lest you think that there's no redemption from your Tink behaviors, I'm here to tell you that you can get rid of Tink and have a healthy sex life with a good man.

Many men have confided in me through the years, particularly during marriage counseling, that the most attractive aspect of any woman is a certain joie de vivre—French for "joy of life"—a positive, life-affirming spark of energy that radiates from a woman's heart and soul. People of all ages are drawn to her, even old people and children.

I believe this spark comes from being connected to the divine source of all energy and light. With that spark comes peace, fulfillment, joy, and a sense of purpose in life, even in the midst of grief or tragedy.

The most attractive thing about a woman—instead of her butt, youth, bra size, or leg length—is the light in her eyes, which shines when the light in her heart burns brightly. Before you think that offering yourself sexually to men is the way to their hearts, think again: it's not your ability in the bedroom that creates healthy relationships. It's your heart.

PART II

Into the Woods

oes your mother get letters?" asked Wendy.

  "Don't have a mother," Peter said. Not only had he no mother, but he had not the slightest desire to have one. He thought them very over-rated persons. Wendy, at once, felt that she was in the presence of a tragedy.

  "Oh, Peter. No wonder you were crying," she said, and got out of bed and ran to him.

  "I wasn't crying about mothers," he said rather indignantly. *"I was crying because I couldn't get my shadow to stick back on. Besides; I wasn't even crying."*

    —J. M. Barrie, *Peter Pan: The Original Story*

CHAPTER 4

Wendy

Loving Lost Boys and Mothering Men

Peter Pan is undoubtedly one of the most popular children's stories ever written, largely because it appeals to the child in all of us who would like to run away from our responsibilities and stay young forever. But like the mature women we are, most of us accept when it is time to grow up and get on with the program of life. Whether we really want to or not, we know it is our job to show up every morning and get the hard stuff done. In fact, having people to care for and love usually makes women feel needed and happy, right?

Like Wendy, however, some of us are a bit *too* responsible. Not only do we deal with our own problems and responsibilities, we tend to take on everyone else's problems as well. We believe that is what we are supposed to do. We mother everyone, *particularly our men*, and believe that is what a woman worth her salt should do if she wants to be a good wife, mother, daughter, or friend.

Taking care of other people *is* a good thing, especially when the people we are caring for are unable to care for themselves. That is what kind and unselfish people do. But a SAM woman with Wendy tendencies takes care of people who are perfectly capable of taking care of themselves, and does so at the expense of her health, sanity, and personal happiness (not to mention the independence of the person she's caring for). She uses mothering to feel important and in control of everything around her. Then she wonders why she feels so angry, tired, and taken advantage of all the time. It's not that she doesn't love her husband and children, but there are other things she'd love to do if she just didn't have so many people to look after all the time.

Many of us find ourselves caught in this situation, not knowing how in the world we became so earthbound. Here we are, strapped into our Playtex Cross Your Heart bras, waiting anxiously for the lift-off that never seems to come. At least Wendy got to fly, but we're stuck down here on the ground, held down by the heavy weight of all the problems we've let others pile on our wings.

There are two big mistakes that a woman with Wendy tendencies makes when it comes to men, and it doesn't matter if she is married or single. Either she is drawn to men who need a mother instead of a partner, or she finds a perfectly good man, yet she treats him like a child. Over time, both types of men end up handing over most of the responsibility for their lives and relationships to her, for entirely opposite reasons. The end result is that she is so busy running everyone else's lives that she has no time or energy for a life of her own.

No matter what your age or marital status, if you are a Wendy, you *can* have the life you want, *if* you will start taking care of yourself. And the first step on that journey begins with the fourth right-romance rule:

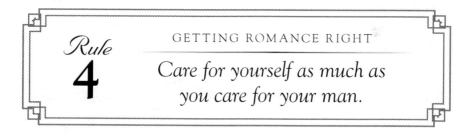

Rule
4

GETTING ROMANCE RIGHT

Care for yourself as much as you care for your man.

Dani's Story

Dani learned the hard way that once you start mothering a man it becomes a way of life that is very difficult to stop. She sought help because she was angry, fatigued, and frustrated, citing that her husband wouldn't step up to the plate and support her.

Dani admitted that she couldn't even go on a business trip without planning her husband's meals, making sure all of his clothes were cleaned and ironed, and calling him every morning to make sure he remembered important appointments. She was worn out before she ever got to her destination because she assumed that it was her job to care for her husband's physical needs, even though her own work in sales was very demanding.

With two young children to care for as well, Dani was becoming increasingly exhausted and angry, and she confided in me that she was considering a divorce.

Dani admitted that her tendency to mother Ted started in high school, because he seemed so vulnerable and alone. His mother had died of cancer when he was a child, and Ted always told Dani she reminded him of his late mother.

The pair dated for a couple of years, and in her senior year in high school Dani learned she was pregnant. Ted was thrilled at the thought of finally having a "real" family of his own, although Dani was overwhelmed at the thought of having a baby so young.

But in spite of her fears, she decided to keep the baby, and the couple married as soon as they both turned eighteen. Once they finished high school and the baby was born, they moved into a small mobile home on the outskirts of town. Fortunately, Ted landed a fairly decent job in town as a car mechanic.

Dani kept house and took care of their baby while Ted worked during the day and attended the local community college at night, getting advanced certifications in mechanics. Dani loved feeling so adult and mature, and she enjoyed the freedom from her own mother and father, even if she and the baby were alone most of the time.

Because Ted was so busy, Dani made most of their major

decisions. He soon depended on her totally to keep his life organized. He confessed he had never learned to manage money and claimed Dani was better at all of that anyway.

But after they had a second child two years later, the two found they couldn't afford for Dani to stay home and not work, especially if they were ever going to be able to buy a house, something they desperately wanted for their future. Once the decision was made, Dani quickly found a job. The pay was good, but the hours were long and often required her to work on weekends. Her mother watched their two little girls during the day, and Ted offered to help out with the domestic responsibilities.

But in spite of the change in their situation and Ted's promises to help, nothing really changed. Ted seemed unaware of the many things that needed to be done, even the most basic chores or spending quality time with their children.

Overwhelmed by all the responsibility, Dani began to take out all of her frustrations on Ted verbally. The minute he walked in the door from work, she would start in on him about helping her. In a rage, he would stomp out of their mobile home, slamming the door, and often disappear for days on end. Dani began to accuse him of being unfaithful, though he claimed he was staying with a friend from work.

We give and give and give—especially to the men in our lives. But contrary to common belief, sometimes we can give too much.

The two reconciled, but Dani continued to shoulder most of the responsibility for the family, and now that Ted is the service manager of a large trucking firm, he travels a great deal as well, still leaving Dani alone much of the time. Dani's situation wasn't hopeless, but she did have some hard work in front of her. Let's look more closely at her story.

Confusing Need with Love

Dani had confused being needed with being loved in her relationship with her husband. After counseling, she realized that she had learned her mothering behavior from her own mom, who never worked outside of the home and doted on Dani's father. Her own father was a tired, passive man who worked long hours at his job on the railroad, so Dani never saw him doing much of anything around the house, except tinkering with an old car in the garage. Her mother confirmed to her, time and time again, that love was found in caring for the domestic details.

Just like Dani, many of us mother our men because we, too, confuse being needed with being loved. Women who are especially competent at nurturing or who have doubts about their worth as women are especially Wendy-prone. In other words, we become codependent.

Codependence is a term that describes people who confuse being needed with being loved. It is a behavior learned from our childhoods, when we learned—either from our own mothers or someone else—that a good way to feel important in the lives of others is to become indispensable to them.

Somewhere along the way, we had difficulty feeling loved unless we were doing something for somebody. In fact, we may have grown up in a situation where the only attention we got was when we were making another person's life easier, or the only way we could keep them happy was to become their overly responsible "little helpers."

So we give and give and give. But contrary to common belief, sometimes we can give too much. When we give through codependency, the more we give, the less we get back. We surround ourselves with people who expect us to give long past our giving-out point. Not only that, they become so used to our mothering that they forget how to take care of themselves.

One of the main characteristics of a girl with Wendy tendencies is that she does all *the mothering* all *the time, even in situations where mothering is not needed.*

We do not realize we are trading our mothering for a form of life insurance and, for the severe codependent, a form of emotional blackmail. We think that if our man is dependent upon us to meet his needs and take care of him emotionally, then he won't leave us.

The ulterior motive underlying our giving is really a fear of being alone and not knowing who we'd be and what we would do with our lives if we weren't mothering someone all the time.

It is an identity issue—we get our sense of self through what we do for others, often to the point where we become addicted to being needed. We desperately need to be needed, because we are terrified that unless we are needed, we will end up alone.

This is especially difficult for women who were born with a strong nurturing instinct anyway. Some of us have a killer mothering instinct, you know. It's in our genes. The brains of women who have this extrastrong instinct actually have higher levels of the hormones that contribute to the ability to nurture others, particularly our young. Of course, it stands to reason that most men don't have high levels of those hormones, because biologically it is not their role to bear young—although according to some recent scientific reports, this may be changing. That will be the day. . . .

In some cases, our habit of mothering our men also arises, as it did in part for Dani, from feelings of incompetence. Having gotten pregnant in high school and marrying so young, Dani always felt she had to prove how competent and intelligent she was by controlling everyone around her. I soon learned that one of the reasons Ted didn't help her around the house was because everything had to be Dani's way all the time. And when Ted tried to help, she always found something wrong with his efforts. So Ted just quit trying.

Many women find it very difficult to give up control, even when they've been complaining about being overworked for years. It is especially hard for women who don't work outside of the home and who see running the house as their job. They see themselves—and want to be seen—as a chief cook and maid service, daily planner and problem solver, that is, until they get sick and tired of being in charge. The trouble is, once they put themselves in that role, it is very hard to change, because others around them want them to stay just like they are!

When we stop doing those things and take positive action to change, everyone's attitudes will change, particularly those of our men. Dani once told me in counseling, rather joyfully, that her husband enjoyed having a happy wife, even if it meant he had to do his own laundry.

Mothering Messages

Unfortunately, our families, our churches, and even our friends may be putting a lot of pressure on us to stay just like we are. As women, we get a lot of conflicting messages from others, particularly from those who benefit most from keeping us in the nurturing mode. Wouldn't we all like someone who cleans up our messes, pays our bills, bakes the casseroles, and keeps the world running? Don't we all need a wife?

Sometimes our own mothers cannot understand why we don't sacrifice our lives for our husbands or boyfriends, because that is what many of them did. They cannot fathom a world where women don't feel it is their responsibility to do all of the nurturing and caretaking, even when we are young daughters and the men we are caring for are fathers, brothers, and boyfriends. Therefore, they may inadvertently make us feel guilty because we don't follow in their paths.

All that said, there *are* times when it is perfectly healthy to mother our partners, especially when they are sick or if they have just suffered an emotional blow. We need to lavish some nurturing love when our man has lost a job, a friend, or a beloved pet. We *all* need mothering at times like these.

But remember, one of the main characteristics of a girl with Wendy tendencies is that she does *all* the mothering *all* the time, even in situations where mothering is not needed.

Stopping the Cycle

Men who end up with mothering wives probably also had overmothering mothers. This is one way the cycle continues, but you have the power to stop this in your own life now and save someone else later. Many women tend to mother their own sons too much—because we are so nurturing, we cannot bear to see them hurting. We clean up their rooms, write their thank-you notes, and call in sick for them when they party too much the night before. Before we know it, they are grown and we are paying off their debts, bailing them out of jail, and trying to protect them from their mistakes. We believe that if we just do it one more time, they will grow up and become the men we hoped they would become.

But the sad truth is that when we overmother—when we create codependent relationships with our sons—we cripple them. They learn that there are no real consequences to immature behavior because someone will clean up after them. Thus, after years of mothering them, we find we still have to mother them well into their adulthood—even if they marry mothering wives (which they will probably do). We continue mothering them while they cheat on their wives, steal from their bosses, and abuse drugs and alcohol. Then we take over raising the children they father, our grandchildren, while we wait for them to get their act together; and the cycle just keeps repeating itself. We eliminate the possibility that we will ever be able to do anything in life but mother others, because we no longer have the time, money, or energy. We become old before our time and worn down by our cares and worries. Imagine the relief we'd feel if we just learned to break that cycle!

> *Do you really enjoy controlling and running your household without help or interference? Are you willing to let go of making all the decisions and not criticize him when he doesn't do everything your way?*

Little Boy Lost

We've discussed why women mother men too much; now we need to look at the men who think they need a mother. Wendy (and those of us like her) seems drawn to immature men who never want to grow up. But it is one thing to fall in love with Peter—at least he had leadership skills. It is another thing altogether to take on a lost boy.

75

Lost boys are just that: truly lost. They are confused, lonely, sad, hurt, and angry, and most of the time, they refuse to take care of themselves. As time goes by, a lost boy will make a Wendy truly miserable.

The Wendy in us longs to hug them, wipe their tears, and fix all their boo-boos. There is just something so *needy* about them. We believe with all of our hearts that if we just love them enough, the power of our love will save them. We comfort ourselves by remembering that we are the only ones who truly understand how deeply wounded and hurt the lost boy is. *No one understands that he didn't have a good mother.*

Lost boys are usually children who are abused and neglected or the products of bitter, broken relationships. They often grow up to become confused and angry adults. If a man has serious issues with his own parents, particularly his mother, you may become the target of all that bottled anger toward women later in his life.

If you are drawn to men like this, dating a man like this, or considering marrying a man like this, you may be in for a rough haul. Unless he has a major spiritual transformation and some good therapy, he is likely not to be a very good husband or father.

If he is well into midlife and still acting like a child, there is an excellent chance he will never grow up. Without a major crisis to force the issue, he will just go from one mothering woman to another—women who will protect him from ever having to face his own fears and inadequacies. The irony is that the very things we find so cute and endearing about lost boys often become the things we detest the most about them later. We can become particularly unhappy with him when we need a good father for our children or someone who can take care of us for a while. The good news is, I think I can help you here. Let's start looking at solutions.

How to Stop Mothering

Change takes time. You won't be able to stop mothering men overnight, especially if you are already with someone you've mothered for quite awhile.

The best thing you can do for your relationship is to start building a *partnership* with your husband or boyfriend, one in which the giving and getting are in relatively equal measure.

The worst thing you can do is use criticism, snide remarks, eye rolling, and excessive talk to attempt to get him to change. That will only make matters worse.

Ultimately, you are going to have to be honest with yourself. Do you really enjoy controlling and running your household without help or interference? Are you willing to let go of making all the decisions and not criticize him when he doesn't do everything *your* way?

You are going to have to communicate to your man in a kind, clear, concise, and firm way that you are going to stop being his mother. You may need to write it down in a letter, in order to state your feelings neutrally, without blame and accusation and without ranting and raving.

I once read that a well-known singer wrote a letter to all the members of her family who were overly dependent on her and who drained her emotionally with all their problems. Her family of origin was very poor, and once she became famous and wealthy, her family saw her as their angel. She didn't elaborate about their problems out of respect for their privacy, but she did say that she let them know that their continual requests for money, time, and intervention were contributing to her rather significant health issues at the time.

That is what happens when we bottle up our feelings, shoulder unnecessary burdens, and try to solve everyone's problems. We get sick, and sometimes the only way to get others to realize just how sick we are becoming is to tell them so in a way that is straightforward and kind, perhaps even in a letter. But you might need to write it then leave it for a week, so you can reread it before giving it to your man or a family member. You want to keep your words free from blame, and you want to initiate positive change, not negative reaction.

The trick is to keep your cool, stay calm, and go about your change systematically. Catch yourself when you jump in giving advice, offering solutions, and taking over in situations where your help is really not needed. Overnurturing actually deprives your husband, boyfriend, family members, or children the chance to learn and grow. After all, we learn from practicing and making mistakes, not from letting others solve our problems for us.

For every situation, examine whether your help is really needed. What would happen if you didn't sign up for that committee, take responsibility for that office party, or listen to that coworker's problems to the point where you are drained and dis-tracted from your own work?

You *can* stop being everyone's mother. You *can* conquer code-pendence. You might not be able to save Peter Pan or a lost boy, but I promise you, you don't have to be his mother anymore, and you can relax for a change.

My heavens, you might even get to fly.

The old queen decided to make sure the princess really was a princess. She knew that only a real princess was truly sensitive and would require perfection. So she hurried to the guest chamber, stripped back the bedclothes, and hid one tiny, hard pea under twenty mattresses. Then she piled twenty feather comforters on top of the twenty mattresses! That night, the princess climbed to the top, and there she slept all night. In the morning they asked her if she slept well. "Oh no, it was terrible!" said the princess. "I scarcely slept at all. I lay on something so hard that I'm black and blue all over!" They could see she was a real princess, now that she had felt one pea all the way through twenty mattresses and twenty feather comforters. So the prince made haste to marry her, because he knew he had found a true princess

—PARAPHRASED FROM THE PRINCESS AND THE PEA,
BY HANS CHRISTIAN ANDERSEN

CHAPTER 5

The Princess and the Pea

The Ultimate Perfect People-Pleaser

Many successful women are high achievers, and in order to be successful, it doesn't hurt to be a little bit of a perfectionist. But in this folk tale, the princess is so perfect she can feel a small pea underneath twenty mattresses and twenty down comforters— a ridiculous standard set by the queen to test her worthiness. And that is exactly the theme of this chapter: the ridiculous standards women set for themselves in their quest to feel worthy, and how that struggle to achieve perfection drives them, right along with the men in their lives, crazy.

Miss Perfect must have every hair, pillow, or dish in its place. Her children are always spit and polished, her husband looks as if he just stepped off the pages of GQ magazine, and you never catch her without her makeup. Her house is always spotless, and she leads every committee in her church and her children's school.

Her nails are manicured and her hair is expertly cut and colored. She exercises daily and her weight is ideal (unless she gets really depressed and goes on an eating binge because she hates not being perfect). Her children make high grades in school (until they rebel and decide to become slobs instead), and her cat is continually in hiding because she vacuums compulsively.

Miss Perfect can be like June Cleaver on steroids—compulsive, miserable, and unhappy no matter what she accomplishes. She is never satisfied with her house, her appearance, her weight, her achievements, her career, or her financial status.

We all know her—many of us *are* her. She's easy to spot because every time you see her and her family, they are photo-op ready: dressed to the nines, squeaky clean, and smiling—even the dog! Oh my goodness, I'm worn out just telling you about her.

But behind the scenes their lives are far from perfect. Women who, like the princess in our fairy tale, live on and breathe perfection, usually struggle with many conflicting feelings, which take a toll on their health and their emotions. In a constant state of restless agitation, the perfection-seeking woman often overworks, worries, and starves herself into depression, chronic fatigue, frequent illness, and difficulties in her relationships.

Many of them come to see me in counseling, secretly of course, and often reveal a whole slew of hidden problems, such as an eating disorder or a husband who is having an affair. When such problems surface, these women often crash into a deep depression, and their lives tend to fall into utter chaos. But they could be so much happier if they would just internalize this next rule:

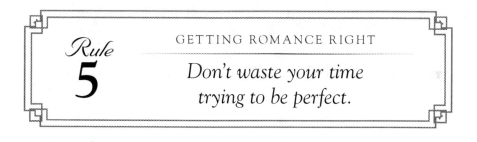

Rule
5

GETTING ROMANCE RIGHT

*Don't waste your time
trying to be perfect.*

Jen's Story

It might help if you hear the story of one of my clients, Jen, age forty-two. I asked her if she'd be willing to write it down for this book, and she agreed. She called it her "diary of a madwoman."

I don't know exactly when it started. I've always been a worrier, even when I was little. I was also neat and particular. Mama and I had fixed my room up real pretty, like a room for a princess, all pink and frilly.

I had a whole bunch of dolls, and they'd sleep in a line next to me in bed. Each night, I would switch them around and let them take turns sleeping next to me. I would even write down where they slept every night so I wouldn't forget whose turn it was. I didn't want one of them to think I played favorites. I guess I was sort of weird about things like that.

My mom got really sick and died when I was a senior in high school. She had cancer, and it took over pretty fast. She was always a hard worker, but when she got sick, I had to look after her and my sisters, since I was the oldest. It was hard, but I knew what I had to do.

My dad started drinking a lot not long after my mom died, but he seemed to do a little better if I cooked and cleaned and looked after things like Mama did, so I did, just to keep the peace. He'd get mad at me anyway, but sometimes when he was drunk, he would cry because he missed Mama so much and tell me how glad he was that I could take her place. So I kept things running as perfectly as I could, hoping for his praise.

I met Derrick right after I graduated from high school, and we got married at Christmas. I couldn't wait to get away from my daddy, but I felt bad about leaving my two sisters, so Derrick let them come live with us. His little boy from his first marriage lived with us, as well as my sisters, so we were kind of crowded, but that was okay.

We rented a cute little fixer-upper in Holly Springs, and I worked hard to make it a home. I was very proud of our little house. But once we were all out of his house, Daddy started drinking even more. It would tear up my nerves, but I was determined that me and my sisters would have a good life in spite of him. My desire to be perfect—and have my sisters be perfect, too—only increased. Finally, his drinking took its toll, and he died of liver disease a few years later.

I sold my parents' house and realized I really enjoyed the process, so I took the money from the sale and earned a real estate license. After that, Derrick and I started a business buying old houses and fixing them up to sell.

We didn't have much money, so we put in a lot of sweat equity—and I do mean sweat. There were nights when I'd be painting and caulking until the wee hours, trying to get everything up to my high standards, then keeping the books and taking care of our own house during the day. But I got it all done somehow.

We started making good money, because there was a housing shortage in Raleigh at the time. We built a beautiful home for ourselves, and I decorated it like you wouldn't believe. Everyone around us would comment on what a wonderful life and family we had.

I honestly can't exactly pinpoint when things started going wrong. Derrick kept complaining about how irritable I was and told me that I needed to slow down and enjoy life. He started getting upset because I'd work so hard and stay up so late; there were many nights I didn't come to bed until long after he was asleep.

Eventually, the recession hit, and the housing market started falling off. We had a lot of houses that wouldn't sell, but you'd better believe the bank still wanted their money every month.

We were way overextended, and my perfectionist tendencies started affecting more than just my marriage.

I was worried sick and started aching and burning all over. The doctor couldn't find anything at first, and then he finally decided I had fibromyalgia. I had a hard time getting out of bed in the mornings. Then one day I woke up, and I literally couldn't get out of bed.

I just lay there crying and crying. It was like this big black cloud had just moved over me out of nowhere. I can honestly say that everything seemed hopeless, especially my marriage.

Derrick got sick of me lying in bed crying. After a while, he got an apartment and moved out. At least I didn't have to worry so much about what he was going to think anymore. We filed bankruptcy, and now I'm trying to get this house sold. I don't know what's going to happen to me next. I just try to take it one day at a time—and try to relax a little. It turns out that even I wasn't perfect enough to hold everything together.

The Perfect Princess

This is a very common story, and it is not limited to married women, those with grief and loss issues, or even those from difficult families or alcoholic parents. In fact, much of the history of the world is built on the blood, sweat, and tears of those who became determined to overcome the obstacles in their lives by hard work and focused determination. But some of us take this determination too far and become confused about what it means to be a wife, mother, and woman. Somewhere along the way, we start equating perfection with success.

There are many clues in Jen's story about where her particular brand of perfectionism started. In her case, it could be traced to her early childhood. This, of course, was complicated by the death of her mother in high school. You'll probably notice that Jen never talked about the effect her mother's death had on her—only how it affected her father. Jen really never grieved for her mother, because her father was doing all the family grieving. She had not allowed herself

> *Perfectionists tend to believe that everything is their fault and that if they can just be perfect enough, they can keep bad things from happening.*

to grieve her father's death, either. **What came out of therapy** was that she felt intensely guilty about how he died. She felt that she could have somehow prevented him from drinking so heavily and dying the way he did if she had just worked harder at being a better daughter.

Do you catch the implications in that statement? Jen's story is just one profound example of how we can develop a *performance orientation* in our approach to life—believing that we can change anything if we just work hard enough. Often, the things we wish we could change are out of our control, such as the deaths of loved ones, estrangements, illness, or the breakup of our families. Our grief is unresolved because it also contains within it an element of guilt and a tendency to dwell on the what-ifs. Perfectionists tend to believe that everything is their fault and that if they can just be perfect enough, they can keep bad things from happening.

Grief and loss often drive us into behaviors that are rigidly controlling, reactionary, and restrictive—especially if we are already perfectionists anyway. We believe that we can outwit our painful memories if we just run fast enough and become successful enough in our chosen spheres. For women, that is most often in their physical appearance, their type of home, and their financial status; and it eventually seeps into their relationships. But our demons always catch up with us, if we don't stop in our tracks and face them head on.

Jen sabotaged her marriage by working herself to the point of exhaustion, focusing on building her career, and keeping up an unreasonable schedule that interfered with the development of emotional intimacy and depth in her relationships. Her early-childhood losses led her to fear abandonment. Later in counseling, her breakthrough moment came when she realized she had actually avoided intimacy with others for fear of losing them. In her mind, it was better to trust in her successes than in the people she loved. But the irony is that the very abandonment she feared came about because her behavior ensured that it would. She drove away the man she loved.

Of course, Derrick was an accomplice in the process, but it was likely he did not realize this. There is a good possibility this marriage could have been saved with an earlier intervention.

Many women exhibit perfectionist tendencies at one time or

the other, but not every woman lets these tendencies ruin her relationship with her partner or allows them to interfere with having a happy life. A bit further along, we will discuss the women who do allow this to happen and how that relates to being stupid about men.

But first we need to discuss the problem in general. We must establish the difference between someone who has perfectionist tendencies and someone who takes perfectionism to the extreme—to the point of being mildly to seriously obsessive-compulsive. If your symptoms are severe, then it becomes a clinical disorder related to a chemical imbalance in the brain.

For the clinically obsessive-compulsive, good medication is available. If you do a lot of counting, excessive cleaning (like washing your hands over and over), or you feel the need to follow strict rituals in order to feel safe, then you may suffer from this disorder and should seek professional therapy. If others worry about you and point out your compulsive behavior, this is a strong indicator that you have a serious medical problem.

Most perfectionists don't have obsessive-compulsive disorder, but many do suffer from depression. Depression often accompanies perfection because it is simply *hard* trying to be perfect all the times. Actually, that's an understatement. Not only is it hard, it is impossible . . . and exhausting, not only for you, but for the men in your life.

The Perfect People-Pleaser

Whether you are obsessive-compulsive, depressed, or simply overly concerned with being perfect, the issues that drive most perfectionists are bound up in two conflicting emotions: pride and fear.

Perfectionists are obsessed with what others think—they are proud individuals ashamed of who they are (it *is* possible to feel both things at once). Both of these emotions can lead us to become attention-seekers who feel anxious and agitated when we are not achieving the unrealistic ideals we have established for ourselves.

Pride is a complicated issue. How *can* we feel both shame and pride at the same time?

From a spiritual perspective, pride is that thing in our minds that elevates us above God and others. It is that selfish, egocentric part of our hearts that secretly believes that we *should* be better than others. However, the perfectionist often has shame issues and is fearful she does not measure up to others. This wounds her pride, forcing her into a cycle of proving herself over and over as a form of suppressing the anxiety that bubbles up each time she questions her performance in any situation. This wounds her *pride*. Shame will not allow her to relax, enjoy life, and become humble and transparent, because she is too focused on hiding her flaws and too fearful that others are going to discover her secrets. Ironically, many perfectionists won't seek counseling because they cannot bear the thought of revealing themselves to another or admitting they have a problem. It doesn't square with their vision of themselves. They see the need for counseling as a terrible weakness that must be kept hidden at all costs. Of all the clients I see, perfectionists are the most consumed with confidentiality and the most anxious that someone will see them coming into my office.

The Perfect Body

One source of conflict that is found in almost every perfectionist woman is shame about her body. Perfectionists are often unable to look into the mirror and, no matter how attractive they are, see anything but their faults—the little lumps, bumps, and imperfections that make us the unique, special woman we really are. To an even higher degree than the average woman, extreme perfectionists crave a perfect body, right along with a perfect everything else in their lives. Many who struggle with perfectionism avoid sex because they don't like to be naked in front of a man—vulnerable to his scrutiny. Some women become addicted to plastic surgery, liposuction, or exercise.

For this reason, a closet full of clothes is never good enough; nothing is suitable. For many, shopping is an anxiety-inducing activity because nothing seems to look or fit right. In that case, it can become tempting to shop compulsively in search of the ideal look. When that happens, the perfectionist can go into debt, and the debt itself can be a source of shame and conflict with her partner.

This dissatisfaction with self is very difficult, on several levels, for the men in their lives. They often don't understand why their compliments and praise aren't enough to assure her that she is attractive, and they question how much she values them, since their opinions don't seem to matter. On the other hand, a perfectionist can wear a man down by continually asking for positive feedback about how she appears. "Does this make me look fat?" or "I hate the way this dress makes me look" become a litany in the day of the man living with a perfectionist. No matter what he says to her, nothing reassures her of her worth and beauty, and that makes him feel frustrated and helpless. After a while, he just gets plain angry.

> *Men, in general, like to "fix" things. So if they cannot make us feel better about ourselves, they start to believe that something is wrong with them because nothing is ever good enough for us.*

Men, in general, like to "fix" things. So if they cannot make us feel better about ourselves, they start to believe that something is wrong with them because nothing is ever good enough for us, never "fixed."

The need to be perfect can also compromise the quality of a couple's sex life. Instead of relaxing and getting into the moment, a perfectionist tends to be so focused on her performance that she cannot enjoy the moment. She observes and analyzes her every move, which acts as an emotional block to achieving orgasm. She often accuses her husband of not being a good lover, or sometimes she becomes so performance oriented that she turns a lovemaking session into a circus act, intent on making it the "perfect experience." That can be exhausting!

The need to criticize and focus on the mistakes of others instead of acknowledging their strengths is one of the ways women derail relationships. In our pride and in our need to prove we are perfect, we can come off as "know-it-alls" who cannot fathom that there are other ways of doing things. It's "my way or the highway" for the perfectionist, because there is only one road to perfection.

Some perfectionists don't realize that their vision actually blinds them to the rights of others. Others feel devalued, marginalized, or minimized in any effort that requires team participation—which is exactly what marriage or any romantic partnership requires. Some partners of perfectionists just give up and let her have her way. Others rebel with petty power struggles or find unhealthy ways to balance power in the relationship.

Again, being a perfectionist has its roots in excessive pride, but it also directly relates to intelligence, talents, and skills. Perfectionists often *are* right about many things. That is what is so infuriating about them. They do things with more flair, innate good taste, and skill than others; and they get a lot of praise for being so excellent in what they do. But they become addicted to hearing the praise that goes along with performing well, whether it is from coworkers, friends, or the public. Ironically, they often discount that praise when it comes from a husband or someone they've been in a long-term relationship with, as they manage to convince themselves that his standards are far too low and that it is their job to bring him up to a higher level.

But sometimes, especially when they cannot keep up the pace, some women with perfectionist tendencies will get angry at what they feel to be the unrealistic expectations of others—not willing to admit that it is they who've raised the bar so high.

Some perfectionists are so regimented and compulsive that they would rather live alone than with someone whom they believe disturbs the sterile order of their lives. This is a choice they make, and it's not necessarily wrong; but it can leave them very alone and lonely. As time goes by, they may realize they could have had a family, children, and lots of adventures had they just been a little less perfect.

The Flip Side of Perfect

There is another side to perfectionism that is the opposite of hyperactivity and overachievement. It is actually possible to be so worried about being perfect that you don't do anything at all, or you procrastinate so badly that your tasks become far more complicated because of delay (like paying your taxes or credit-card balances.)

Perfectionists who fear failure can actually *freeze*, like a deer caught in the headlights of a car. This fear response leads us to play all sorts of mind games, rationalizing our delays or distracting ourselves with less-important activities.

At this point, being a practically paralyzed perfectionist (*say that five times fast*) makes her run in circles instead of progressing forward. She will waste a lot of time doing nonessential things because she cannot face the things that *are* important. She will obsessively clean her house when she should be enrolling in a college course, or she'll be rigorously dieting and tanning when she knows she should really be getting some lab work done or having that lump in her breast checked out.

Again, this is very hard on a relationship with a man, especially when bills don't get paid or he sees the woman he loves not taking care of her health because she is so consumed with her appearance. In any joint financial arrangement, her excessive worry, fear, and paralysis in the face of financial stress may also serve to undermine his own confidence in his abilities to provide for his family. But don't worry, all you Princess and the Pea perfectionists! The good life is still yours for the taking.

Becoming Im-Perfectly Happy

It may seem hard to believe, but it *is* possible to relax, enjoy life, and stop driving yourself and your man crazy making everything fit your vision of perfection. One way to do that is to let go of perfection one step at a time.

The husband of one of my clients once told me that he watched his wife pick up a decorative pillow on the sofa and plump it every time she walked through their den.

He had asked her numerous times to just leave the pillow alone, and he was exasperated because she refused to budge on the topic, even though she had expressed that the exercise was tiring. But in her mind, she had explained, the room would not have looked right without that perfect decorator pillow perched at just the right angle on the end of the couch.

Her many self-imposed efforts at perfection exhausted and overwhelmed her (she was also very codependent). The husband was upset because she spent so much time creating the perfect home, she had no real time for quality relationships, and often was much too tired for sex. Sometimes she even fell asleep during lovemaking.

In counseling, I went back to that pillow. I asked her to take one step toward letting go by putting the pillow in a closet for one week. I asked if it was more important for her family to be happy or for her home to be perfect. She agreed that she was ready for her family to be happy and that removing the pillow was a good place to start.

She took another step toward letting go through a game that she and her family began to play. For fifteen minutes each day (often in the evening before bed), the whole family would clean the house together. The only rule was that she could not criticize how it was done or go behind her family and improve on their work, especially in space that belonged to others (like her children's rooms, her husband's office, and so on). They set up family awards and prizes, so everyone got involved.

This helped my client with her feelings of being overwhelmed, but it also taught her how to be less critical and demanding, to relax her standards a bit, and to have fun for a change. She had to accept that the purpose of the clean-up game was to show that they could get the job done *as a family*, without adhering to an unrealistic standard of perfection.

Another way to move beyond perfectionist tendencies is to *slow down*. Most perfectionists tend to be addicted to their own stress, anxiety, and adrenaline. Many of us feel anxious if we don't have some impending deadline or major challenge. Staying busy makes many women feel important, necessary, and keeps us from thinking about the things that worry us.

We may be the fastest, but that doesn't mean that we are headed anywhere in particular. We can be pedaling hard on that great hamster wheel of life, but it doesn't matter how fast we go or how good we look if we are going around in circles.

We perfectionists must also learn how to *care less about what others think*. On an innate level, perfectionism is all about caring too much about the opinion of others. The truth is, if you want to be happy, it will be essential that you practice ignoring what others may think. You can begin the process slowly and in small ways—like not wearing makeup to the grocery store. You will be surprised how freeing it is to be yourself, without worrying if your flaws are showing. You will also be amazed at how much your man loves you just as you are, and that awareness will make you more free in your love

> *If you want to be happy, it will be essential that you practice ignoring what others may think.*

life. If you are not married, guys will be attracted to your easy self-confidence and your relaxed self-acceptance.

We are all designed for equality in the world, regardless of how we look, how thin we are, or how much money we make. Good grief, if I was focused on any of those things, I would not be a therapist, and I would certainly not have written this book. But if you want to know the truth, for many years I *was* a perfectionist, and that kept me from doing many of the things I wish I had tried earlier. It also made life difficult for my husband and children, because they felt I was overly critical and demanding. So trust me, I know how freeing it is to cut loose, accept yourself as you are, and get on with life.

I am continually surprised at the sheer number of women I meet who have convinced themselves that they cannot do anything of any real significance because they are slightly overweight, don't have enough money, are too short, too tall, or don't have enough education.

But if you look at some of the most influential women in the world, you'll notice that not a single one is by any means perfect. They do things in spite of their flaws and obstacles. They have learned to turn their handicaps into strengths—this is what we love most about them, and *this* is one of the key lessons we must learn from them. Instead of trying to appear to be perfect, they deliberately play up their imperfections, like their imperfect bodies, families, and business failures. Think about Oprah, Whoopi Goldberg, and Rachel Ray. Even Martha Stewart has seemed to relax a great deal since going to prison. She is teaching us that being flawed and imperfect is simply human, not fatal. Being imperfect actually means that we are fully alive.

The greatest truth is this: we need only the approval of God—

who offers his favor freely. All others are simply not that important, not even our parents, husbands, boyfriends, or bosses. We don't need to prove that we are royalty (like the princess with her stupid pea) by being offended if someone doesn't meet the standards of our fine-tuned sensibilities. We are already royalty in God's eyes, just as we are.

*O*nce upon a time there was a miller who lived in a poor little village with his beautiful young daughter. He was very ambitious, greedy, and always looking for a way to better himself in society. He decided to take his daughter to the castle, in hopes that she would become a servant there.

When he arrived at the castle, the king's head butler asked the poor miller what talent his daughter had that would make her suitable to serve in the court. The miller, dumbfounded by the splendor of his surroundings, stuttered and lied: "My daughter can spin gold from straw!" Amazed, but rather skeptical, the head butler sent a message to the king, so that he could determine this matter for himself. The king locked the young girl in a castle with a pile of wheat straw in order to reveal the truth one way or the other.

The young girl was distraught, knowing if she did not spin the straw into gold, her father would be put to death.

—FROM RUMPELSTILTSKIN,
TOLD BY THE BROTHERS GRIMM

CHAPTER 6

The Gold-Spinning Maiden

The Girl Who Spun Tales

This story is so delicious—chock-full of symbols, metaphors, and meanings related to women and the secrets they keep to protect themselves and others. In this case, the girl's father tells a bald-faced lie that results in his daughter being locked away in a tower. And like good little girls are sometimes trained to do, she tries—and lies—to protect him.

The remainder of the tale describes a deal the young maiden strikes with a demonic little man who pops up out of the floorboards while she lies on the straw bemoaning her fate. He promises to spin the straw into gold for her if she will give him her firstborn. She agrees, fools the king, and he marries her, believing she can truly spin gold. She assumes her problems are over.

But years later, when her first child arrives, sure enough, the creature returns. The queen cries for mercy, and with relish he concocts a game whereby she must tell him his true name, which is Rumpelstiltskin. With the help of her huntsmen, who hear Rump dancing in the forest and, like an idiot, singing his own name, she discovers his true identity. Screaming foul epitaphs, the enraged little demon drops back down through the floorboards, never to be seen again.

Of course, because it's a fairy tale, from that point on the queen lives happily ever after. The story nonetheless serves as a great illustration of the mistakes we make when we keep secrets and lie so that we can protect our loved ones and ourselves. And in the maiden's case, she not only lied to protect herself and her father, but also to rise in social status.

But secrets and lies can gain a terrible power over us, if we let them, and they can be especially toxic to our relationships with men. That's why we need this sixth right-romance rule:

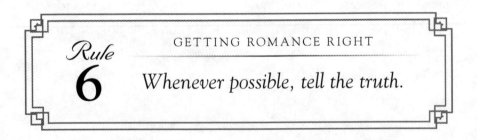

GETTING ROMANCE RIGHT

Rule
6

Whenever possible, tell the truth.

Mindy's Story

Sometimes, as you'll see with Mindy, keeping secrets can almost cost us our lives, as well as our self-respect and opportunities for meaningful relationships.

When Mindy was eight years old, her parents divorced. This was not a surprise to her, as she had never known a time when they had not fought, yelled, or argued with each other. When they finally ended their marriage, Mindy was almost relieved. She remained in the custody of her mother and visited her father every other weekend.

This arrangement worked fine for a couple of years, until her father announced that he had accepted an offer of a new job in a different state. After her father moved, her relationship with him grew more and more distant over time. She attempted on multiple occasions to contact him, but he rarely returned her phone calls or e-mails, his energies evidently being consumed by a new younger wife and their baby.

In the meantime, her mother remarried a man with two boys—one who was three years older than Mindy and another about her age. They all moved into a bigger house, and their life as a family seemed ideal. Mindy tried not to think much about her father and told her mother that she didn't want to spend time with him, anyway.

Mindy's older stepbrother, Kyle, was a good-looking soccer player and very popular at school. As she moved into puberty, she developed a crush on him that was painfully obvious to everyone.

He acted civilly toward her but was annoyed by her obvious adoration and avoided her as much as possible.

One summer day while swimming in her backyard pool with a group of friends, Mindy began showing off to get Kyle's attention. Several times he asked her to "lay off," but her behavior only escalated. Finally, when she began throwing water at him, he rudely shoved her away and told her to leave him alone. Other boys in the pool began making fun of Mindy, and she was horribly embarrassed. As they laughed and jeered at her, she ran to her room, crying all the way.

Humiliated by the incident and her own behavior, and knowing what it would mean for her social status at school, Mindy began to live almost exclusively in her room. She had a television and was allowed to eat her meals there, as her mother was often busy with her career. Mindy's weight began to soar, and two years later, by the age of fourteen, she weighed nearly two hundred pounds.

Mindy quickly became miserable with the way she looked. Her mother threatened to send her to "fat camp" and refused to buy her new clothes unless she lost weight.

Obsessed with becoming thin, Mindy attempted every diet known to man, but with little result. She would lose a few pounds then gain them all back, plus more.

One day, watching a Lifetime movie, she learned how to binge and purge. Though the practice disgusted her at first, she soon became dependent on it as a way to control her eating. Every day revolved around managing how to eat all she wanted without gaining weight. Her secret purging began to dominate her life.

Mindy's mother was thrilled at her daughter's weight loss and bought her a whole new wardrobe to encourage her, unaware of her real problems with food. Mindy continued to binge eat and purge, but she hid the candy wrappers and pizza boxes so no one would find them. No one asked questions when she disappeared to the ladies room in the middle of a meal. No one guessed her secret, even though she was becoming rather thin and her hair began to dull.

This continued all the way into college, where she began partying in earnest. Soon she was dating several boys at a time and drinking rather heavily on the weekends.

But by the following summer, her purging, drinking, and all-night partying had begun to take its toll. She finally sought medical help for ulcers in her mouth; she was weak and suffered from constant colds and sore throats. A nurse helped Mindy admit to her history of purging, drinking, and risky sexual behaviors and referred her to counseling. She was diagnosed with malnutrition, dehydration, and a sexually transmitted disease—all playing terrible havoc with her immune system.

Through therapy, Mindy learned to control her eating disorder and realized that she had a pattern of sabotaging her relationships because she expected to be rejected. She would act out, show off, and end a relationship with a boy as soon as he showed any real interest in her. In other words, she dumped them before *they* could dump her.

In a few moments we'll look at *why* Mindy kept secrets, cut relationships short, and acted out when around boys; but first we need to consider the different kinds of secrets women keep and what those secrets do to our lives.

Different Kinds of Secrets

People of all ages, both male and female, come to me all the time and confess a myriad of secrets they've never told, even though it may have been years since the incidents happened. Whether it was because of something they were ashamed of, as in Mindy's case, or something done to them, the weight and worry of it can become a heavy burden.

Mindy's obvious secret was her eating disorder. But, in a sense, that was only the symptom of her real secret—the divorce of her parents, the loss of relationship with her father, and the inability to get male attention in positive ways. If we are not careful, we can make the mistake of trying to cure the symptom instead of the root problems underneath them.

Of course, Mindy didn't give up her secret about her eating disorder until it turned on her and ravaged her body. But this is not a clinical discussion of the nature and reasons for eating disorders or of other symptoms that the darker secrets in our lives bring about. This is about how Mindy and women like her bury their emotions and lie to themselves and others about their feelings. It is the emotions that are eating them up inside.

To be fair, most women usually keep the darkest of secrets because they're afraid that if the secrets come to light, the truth will tear apart their family or their way of life. And sometimes, that happens. Whether these secrets involve past abuse, family secrets (like the gold-spinning girl), infidelities, eating disorders, or ethically compromising situations they feel they cannot resolve or escape, bringing them to light can devastate lives. I've counseled children who've told their secrets, and as a result, their parents split, someone went to jail, or they suffered any number of traumatizing results. I've even dealt with stupid parents who actually blamed the children for revealing their secrets.

Because we are afraid that something bad will happen if we tell the truth, we keep secrets from people, and especially from the men we love. But it is almost always more harmful to keep secrets than it is to reveal the truth, and that harm usually increases the longer we wait.

In some cases, we keep secrets in order to protect the men we love. And keeping secrets for the sake of our man is tricky— particularly if we are trying to shield him from the consequences of his own harmful behaviors, like alcohol abuse, drugs, or other illegal activity. True, we run the risk of losing him if we don't keep his secrets, but we will find no refuge by staying in a relationship where we are held hostage to our loved one's damaging activities. Why should they ever change if we keep their secrets, protect them from scrutiny, and keep the world turning for them? That is what we professionals call *enabling*. Not only do we enable the behavior, but we enable the loved one to stay stagnant and continue unhealthy actions.

Of course, not all of the secrets we keep are deep and dark. Sometimes the secrets are just bad habits we've learned somewhere along the way, either as children or adults. We somehow learned that it was easier to lie than to tell the truth.

When our secrets are borne from "bad" or embarrassing lifestyle choices—or simply because we want to put forth an idea about ourselves that differs from who are truly are—they usually begin as small "white lies." But over time, lying about small things becomes a habit that is hard to shake. We find ourselves exaggerating, embellishing, and outright lying, mostly because it feels easier or more exciting than the truth. Eventually, secrets that hide truths about ourselves can catch up with us, usually because we forget that we lied and end up contradicting ourselves, or because we have to tell new lies to cover our tracks. After a while, we can't even remember what we've lied about, and we find ourselves having to explain why we didn't tell the truth initially. That can be embarrassing. The irony of it is that, in the long run, lying doesn't make things easier, even little white lies. We can save ourselves a whole lot of trouble if we just tell the truth from the start.

Over time, lying about small things becomes a habit that is hard to shake.

Secrets Always Come to Light

Our deceptions *will* catch up with us. As with the heroine of our folk tale, that little demon eventually pops up and demands his due—often when we least expect it.

Though it may take many years, the stuff hidden inside the walls of our hearts becomes visible from the outside as well. And when our walls start to crack, we are forced to either deal with our issues or stuff them down to an even darker place.

In this chapter's folk tale, the young maiden made a pact with a demonic figure to protect her father. She captured the heart of the king, but in truth, she entered into a life of bondage. The story doesn't say how many nights she lay awake during her pregnancy terrified that the demon would return for her baby, or how many times after her marriage she was accused by the king of lying to him because she could no longer spin straw into gold.

We can learn a valuable lesson from the gold-spinning woman. There's no doubt the woman was trapped by her father's lie. But what's more implicit in the story is the passivity she exhibited in the face of a horrible lie and her willingness to go along with the scheme without seeking any other positive solutions. Perhaps, if she had believed in herself, she could have offered the king an alternative talent to spinning

Not telling the truth can prevent us from working on making changes or from moving toward a healthy and positive future.

gold. The fact that she worked so hard to maintain her secret speaks to a lack of self-worth and confidence in her true self. And when we don't value who we are or are ashamed of ourselves, like the gold-spinning woman or Mindy, we often self-sabotage and end up hurting ourselves more than anyone. We mess things up for ourselves, because we believe our life is going to mess up anyway.

In fact, sometimes the worst secret we keep is how we feel about our own past actions—our shame, guilt, or anger over any number of issues we've dealt with. When we make mistakes, we keep them a secret, not just to protect others, but because we are too ashamed of ourselves to tell what we have done. But not telling can prevent us from working on making changes or from feeling good about ourselves and moving toward a healthy and positive future.

It takes a lot of emotional energy to keep secrets. They make us feel unclean and undermine our view of ourselves as women of worth. They become part of our negative self-image. We don't like others who lie; consequently, we don't like ourselves.

When we don't like ourselves, it is very difficult to relate to healthy men. Even if we are fortunate enough to find a good man, secrets often lead us into doing things that hurt him. Sometimes that is because we don't feel we deserve him or we don't know how to be straight up and honest with him. As a result, we keep things from him that come out later anyway, and we hurt him—and ourselves—far worse than if we'd told the painful truth up front.

But we often remain unaware of our own inner turmoil. Either male or female, one of the things we all become adept at denying is that anything is wrong with us. We become so good at pretending that we even manage to fool ourselves. That is called *denial*.

Not a River in Egypt

Denial (not "the Nile") is a *defense mechanism*, and while we all engage in it at one time or another to a minor degree—no matter how smart, mature, or emotionally stable we are—those who harbor secrets use denial as a daily shield. The behavior is called a defense mechanism because it makes us feel safe in our own little world, especially if we feel unready to face difficult facts about our lives.

To be fair, in some cases denial can be a comforting tool, particularly if you are in a situation you know you cannot change no matter how hard you try. And sometimes, denial is just what you need to manage the unmanageable, without going totally crazy in the process. The old "rose-colored glasses" come in quite handy from time to time.

But if we escape too much, pretend too much, and lie to ourselves when we are insecure or afraid, denial can turn into our very worst enemy. Mindy dealt with her father's abandonment, her mother's criticism, and her shame over her childhood crush by binging, purging, and partying. The very things she turned to for comfort as a child became the poison that made her sick in adulthood.

There's no question that admitting the harmful nature of our secrets—not to mention transparently expressing them—is hard and can feel impossible for women who've made a habit of keeping secrets and telling lies. But this behavior can and must be unlearned, because it damages our belief in ourselves and undermines the trust others have in us.

How do we "unlearn" secret harboring? We unlearn it by first righting as many wrongs as we can and then making a promise to ourselves, to whatever extent possible, never to do it again. We can join support groups, or we can practice disclosure with a wise person who can help us think of less destructive ways to reveal truths or make a decision about whether to disclose the truth.

Artful Disclosure

Okay. So there are some things from your past you need to deal with but don't quite know how. When is it time to tell someone, and how do you do it so the sky doesn't fall? There is an "art" to disclosure, and the *way* we reveal truths is the key to telling our secrets properly.

Sometimes women make the mistake of first talking with a friend or family member. That can blow up in their face if they are not careful. Friends and family members can often be too close to you and to others involved and may not react in a way that is constructive. A pastor or priest may be your best option, or someone outside of your family whom you know can be objective. Sometimes it's helpful to disclose your secret in a letter, so you can carefully determine how to express what you need to say.

To be safe (and I know you might get tired of hearing this), it is always best to discuss disclosure with a licensed counselor before you do anything. They are bound by laws of confidentiality, and you won't run the risk of having your secrets be front-page news before you get some straightforward personal advice on whom and how to tell. They can usually help you evaluate whether you are about to do something too soon, too late, for the wrong reasons, or in a manner that is destructive.

When making a decision about disclosing secrets of any kind, the rule of thumb should be the "law of the greater good." When making any kind of moral or ethical decision, you have to think about what will be best for everyone relevant to the situation, including yourself—*especially yourself!*

And most of the time, the greatest good we can do for ourselves, our partners, and our families is to be honest about who we are, what we've done, or what has happened to us. Even if it causes great pain for a short while, in the end it will be the healthiest thing for everyone. Every woman has to make her own decision about that.

We need to talk a moment about revealing the truth of abuse. If you are in pain over past (or current abuse), you need to tell in spite of whom it hurts. Telling is necessary for your healing. It will help you put the painful event in the past and get on with your life. Revealing a secret about abuse is always for the greater good, because as long as you harbor the secret, the abuser has the potential to continue to hurt you and hurt others.

I know that you don't want to hurt family or friends or break up marriages—and that is understandable. But you owe it to yourself to expose your abuser. You don't have to tell the whole world, but you must tell someone. You cannot be a sacrificial lamb so that others can live happy lives while you quietly crumble inside in order to protect them.

And even if the abuser has passed away, you still need to tell someone. Many women believe that once the abuser is dead then so is the past. But anything that has the power to traumatize us (either physical, verbal, or sexual) remains alive in our minds, as fresh as the day it happened. The only way you can put it in the past is to get it out.

If you have powerful memories of abuse that you relive in your mind all the time, this is a sign that you have suffered a trauma. You need a specialist in trauma therapy—someone who understands that simply talking about the abuse over and over in therapy sessions may actually deepen your trauma. A certified trauma specialist or someone trained in therapies that deal specifically with traumatic stress related to sexual abuse is the best option.

I also must advise you that if you know a child who is being harmed in any way, federal and state law requires that you reveal that information to local law enforcement or social services. You can reveal information like this anonymously, without divulging how you know it. If it comes to light that you knew information of this nature and failed to report it, you could be considered an accessory to the abuse.

Never report a case as a way to strike out at the father, other family members, a boyfriend, or a neighbor. This is very dishonest and could cause a great deal of unnecessary pain for you and the persons you falsely accuse. However, if you have reason to believe a child is being harmed, always err on the side of caution. Don't make the mistake of trying to protect a man or family member you love. You will be causing a child irreparable harm.

But there are some kinds of secrets that are wise to keep. If we feel guilty about something we did a long time ago and just want to unburden ourselves, telling might be an act of selfish destruction. Sometimes a secret may simply be our cross to bear. I've known people who confessed to an old love affair many years after it happened. In a fit of guilt and self-recrimination, they admitted their mistake. However, this just compounded the damage and wounded their spouse unnecessarily.

There are some times when telling does more damage, particularly if a secret has been harbored for a long time and has no power in the present. There are some who would say that a secret always has an undermining power, and that is probably true. But wisdom dictates you to decide if the power is enough to risk destroying your relationship with your husband for the rest of your life. It may simply be best to let the past die, especially if you have asked God for forgiveness and changed your ways.

What if you've never had an affair, but you have random thoughts of infidelity (you didn't know I knew that, did you?) that you don't act on? In most cases it would be selfish to tell your spouse and cause needless pain for him. Instead of feeding your fantasies, try to observe yourself and figure out *why* you are thinking about other men. Work on the relationship you have, instead of fantasizing about what you don't have. That is a better alternative to nursing the fantasies that eventually might have a negative impact on your marriage.

If it is any reassurance, most women think thoughts like this off and on throughout their marriages—that is no deep, dark secret— even if they are in healthy marriages and deeply in love with their mates. It is what you do with your secret thoughts that counts. Do you harbor them and let them grow, or do you show them the door? If you want to keep your relationship intact, I'd suggest the latter.

And, on a side note, please realize that having an "emotional affair" can be just as damaging to a relationship as a sexual affair, if not more so. Guard your heart, girlfriends. Don't talk about your intimate personal emotions with a man outside your marriage. If you are single, don't get personal with a married man. If you can't talk to your man about what is in your heart, you need a counselor, not another male friend.

The truth is, even secrets that we wisely keep need the pure light of honesty shined upon them—even if that means simply being honest with ourselves. But most secrets cannot be kept if we expect to outwit the forces of darkness (like Rumpelstiltskin) that collude to keep us bound in our anger, pain, and fear. The only healthy thing to do is to bring the secret to light and trust that the honesty will bring healing. You may not be able to change the past, but you can shape the future.

> *The only healthy thing to do is bring the secret to light and trust that honesty will bring healing.*

You'll be pleased to know that Mindy was finally able to share her heart, and in time, her health and her relationship with her father were restored. It took a couple of years, but when she was finally able to share her pain with her father, he was able to acknowledge his neglect of her and his regret that he'd caused her so much pain.

I cannot guarantee that you will get the same results if you tell the truth. I'll never promise "happily-ever-after" or a fairy-tale life. What I can promise is that you will feel clean again; you will feel whole. You might lose some relationships, but that may just be a consequence of your past. Plus, with a new approach to honest living, good friendships are just around the corner. God wouldn't ask you to give up something good and then replace it with something bad.

Tell your secrets. Trust God to bring you through the process. It'll be worth it, because when you look in the mirror at the end of the day, you will like what and *who* you see.

PART III

Down in the Soggy, Boggy Swamp

*O*nce upon a time one lovely spring day, a princess sat by a pond near her castle playing with her beloved golden ball. She accidentally dropped the ball into the pond, and she began to cry.

Suddenly, a voice asked, "Your Highness, why are you crying?" She saw that the voice came from a frog who was sitting nearby on a lily pad, and she jumped up in disgust.

The frog said, "I will get your ball for you if you promise to let me eat off your plate and sleep on your pillow tonight."

Repulsed, the princess finally agreed, reasoning that once they were in the castle, she could do what she wished. After all, she was a princess, and he was just a frog.

That evening the frog ate off her plate. But when it came time to go to bed and he hopped on her pillow, the princess was revolted. She picked him up and threw him across the room, and he splattered against the wall.

But instead of a dead frog, there stood a handsome prince. He crossed the room and took the shocked princess in his arms. So the princess pledged her heart to the prince.

—RETOLD FROM *THE FROG AND THE PRINCESS,*

A SEVENTEENTH-CENTURY FOLK TALE

CHAPTER 7

The Frog and the Princess

Do You Think You Can Really Change Him?

This folk tale is a plain-as-day example of how so many women promise to bring a "frog" into their lives—even into their beds—when they have no intention of accepting him as he is. It's enough to make a girl want to croak, because the sad truth is, our true feelings eventually come out, and we end up revealing our frustrations in an ugly display.

Our storybook princess is so repulsed by her frog that she tries to kill him by throwing him against a wall. Splat! And then he magically turns into a wonderful prince. How convenient.

In hopes that you don't resort to such drastic measures, try to remember this rule:

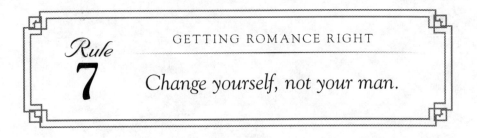

GETTING ROMANCE RIGHT

Rule
7

Change yourself, not your man.

For women, little is surprising about this folk tale. Well, maybe the part where the princess chucks the frog against the wall—that's a bit radical—but the fantasy that an ordinary man can turn into a prince is one we're all familiar with.

By the way, the frog metaphor isn't about wealth or social position. The frog is any man who can never be good enough for the woman he loves. A SAM woman marries a frog—who is often a good man—pretending that she'll love him as he is. But she soon tires of his frog ways. Rather than throwing him against the wall, however, she makes it a personal project to unleash his prince potential. Even if he is a perfectly good frog, she tries to change him into the prince of her dreams.

The Frog and the Princess serves as a cautionary tale about the dangers of blithely assuming we can change a man by the power of our will. When we do that, we run the risk of losing a loving good man, or we drive the one we have crazy trying to turn him into a man he was never intended to be.

Shannon's Story

Shannon and Mark met at the party of a mutual friend. Mark was a senior business major, and Shannon was a junior studying art history. Shannon was attracted to Mark's quiet, serious demeanor. He made her feel safe and protected. In return, Mark was mesmerized by Shannon's vivacious personality, wit, and intelligence.

The two moved into an apartment together after Mark graduated and began working for a local accounting firm. Shannon was not quite sure she was ready to live with Mark, but her ongoing financial struggles, brought on by her parents' recent divorce, made the move seem like the most reasonable thing to do. Mark earned a good salary and could support the two of them, and he felt like a hero since he could provide a stable home for Shannon during her financial and personal difficulties.

The arrangement seemed ideal for about a year. Shannon studied and went to class during the day while Mark worked, and the two would watch television in the evenings or have a few beers with friends.

Shannon graduated the following May, and Mark presented her with a diamond ring as her graduation present. Speechless, Shannon took the ring, but told Mark that she was far from ready to set a wedding date. This didn't matter to Mark—he was just happy that she agreed to marry him at all. Mark loved her deeply and couldn't imagine his life without her. Shannon, on the other hand, found Mark to be a bit stuffy and predictable.

Even so, he was endearing, and she took the ring in the hopes that, over time, Mark would loosen up and be more fun.

But as the summer progressed and her efforts to "improve" Mark didn't seem to change things, Shannon became quiet and irritable. Still seeing him as rather boring and unexciting, Mark now seemed unable to do anything right. She made fun of him in a sort of teasing way in front of friends and questioned why he didn't want to do something more interesting in life.

She hated the way he dressed and was continually trying to get him to try newer, more contemporary styles. Mark preferred the khakis, navy blazers, and golf shirts that were the standard fare in his closet. Shannon often ridiculed the way he looked and told everyone that he was "her accountant."

By the fall, Shannon had landed a part-time job as the manager of a local art gallery, and her attitude and positive regard for Mark improved somewhat. She realized he had many positive qualities, and though she wasn't madly in love with him, thought she might grow to love him more with time. When Mark surprised Shannon by suggesting that they buy a condo together, Shannon become more hopeful that Mark might be capable of giving her the spontaneity she needed in life. Still somewhat reticent about their future together, she agreed. Shannon couldn't resist the opportunity to exercise her decorating skills and transform the place into the upbeat, contemporary living space she imagined.

Once the sale was complete, Shannon busied herself with decorating. Mark expressed pride in how Shannon transformed the aging condo and was amazed at the unique ideas she had incorporated into their wedding plans. By now Shannon felt better about her future with Mark and agreed to set a wedding date.

The wedding was beautiful. But, unfortunately, the marriage was not. A few months afterward, both were in my office for marriage counseling, and the prognosis did not look good.

It started a few days after the honeymoon. Shannon and Mark returned from their cruise to find that the roof on their home had leaked badly, and much of their new furniture and an expensive rug were damaged. Shannon, who had exhausted herself planning the wedding, fell apart, yelling and screaming at Mark for talking her into the condo and telling him she regretted the marriage. Mark, badly shaken, left for the evening. Shannon cried all night.

The next morning, Shannon called her attorney. The attorney talked her into counseling, and that is how she ended up in my office. The hard truth came out quickly: there were no major secrets or traumas complicating Shannon's relationship or life. She simply did not love Mark.

She cared about him a great deal, but he annoyed her terribly. He was tired at the end of the day and wanted a quiet evening by the television, she was geared up by night and wanted to go to gallery openings, new restaurants, and out dancing with friends. She had believed these things would change over time, especially if she exposed Mark to new friends and new ideas; but her attempts to change his basic personality failed. Mark was still the same person she had first met in college, and she realized she had no desire to spend the rest of her life with him if he couldn't become the kind of man she wanted.

Shannon eventually confided that three weeks before the marriage, she'd run into an old boyfriend from college, had a few drinks, and went back to his apartment. After a lot of flirting and another beer, she barely found the wherewithal to resist having sex with him. She left, intending to forget about it, but he started contacting her constantly. She ignored his text messages and e-mails and resumed planning her wedding. She was mortified by what had happened and tried to push it out of her mind, nervous about the e-mails she continued to receive from the other man.

Shannon had desperately hoped that marriage would resolve her ambivalence and the two could be happy. But when she came for her first session with me, she was determined to get a divorce, and she had resumed contact with the ex-boyfriend.

Shannon's life and emotions were a mess. She realized that she had made a terrible mistake by moving in with Mark in the first place. She should have ended the relationship much earlier. Shannon now hated herself for hurting a man who had been so good to her and who obviously loved her very much.

She had believed that over time he would begin to enjoy the same things she did and that she could change the things about him that annoyed her. But that was not the case, and she was sad that she'd ever thought she could. The two are now divorced and have gone their separate ways. Shannon returned the diamond and requested nothing in financial settlement. She continues in therapy, but Mark has taken an accounting job in a different city.

Shannon was in a dilemma many women face these days, especially those of us in a transition phase that makes it difficult for us to support ourselves. It becomes so easy to latch on to a "lifeboat" that will help bring us to a safe shore.

We subconsciously believe, like the princess, that once we get what we need, we can gently disengage and neither party is the worse, not figuring in the probability that we will become more deeply involved than we thought possible. But instead of ending the relationship honestly before any harm is done, we move forward, either because it is easier or because each new development (like a diamond, house, or cruise) is just too much to resist. And if he is reasonably attractive, sweet, and kind, we might find it almost impossible to say good-bye. So . . . many of us do as Shannon did: we blindly plow forward, hoping for the best, trying hard not to dwell on negative outcomes—even though we know our personalities and personal tastes are far too different.

Some of us use "frogs" to get us through times in our lives when we are emotionally unstable, immature, or "just going through a life crisis." We feel we need a stable, secure man who makes us feel safe—a plain, ordinary, dependable guy—like the frog. Instead of being an equal life partner, in many ways he becomes more like our father.

But once the crisis has passed and we've grown up a bit or gotten a prescription for Prozac, our situations don't seem so dire, and we are better able to live on our own. That is when living with a frog can feel confining and unnatural. That is when we tend to try to change him into the man we really want him to be—someone more exciting, more spontaneous, or more . . . you fill in the blank.

Together but Not Satisfied

Women's dissatisfaction with their partners and subsequent attempts to mold and make them into the men they want was the subject of my first book, *Trapped in the Magic Mirror*. It is a problem that I felt deserved the attention of a whole book, and is too complicated to go into here from a deep therapeutic perspective.

But suffice it to say, our inclination to change a man almost always stems from *our desire to be something more than we are.* Women want men who take them places in life that they fear they cannot go on their own. Shannon had all the flair, talent, and artistic skills, but the truth was that she was too flighty and unpredictable to hold down a job. She expected Mark to be a stable anchor who provided an income so she could dabble in her art. But once she was married, the anchor began to feel like an albatross, in spite of the fact that Mark was a very good man who probably would have made a wonderful husband.

When our men do not change on a dime, we frequently resort to all sorts of behaviors that are unhealthy, as Shannon did. More often than we would like to admit, we nag, tease, manipulate, throw temper tantrums, and make fun of our men in an effort to shame him into improving.

This serves no purpose but to discourage them and back them into a corner. In fact, the more we attempt to change our men, the more they resist. A power struggle ensues, and a *toxic communication cycle* of mutual verbal abuse can sometimes result.

In general, the cycle is a pattern of power struggle that typically looks like this: we attack, accuse, blame, and criticize our man, and in turn, he withdraws to self-protect. His withdrawal only increases our anxiety, and we go on the offensive even more, and the withdrawal of our partner becomes worse. Not only worse, but he begins to deliberately do the things that annoy us, just to keep a sense of power in the relation-

> *When our men do not change on a dime, we nag, tease, manipulate, throw temper tantrums, and make fun of them in an effort to shame them into improving.*

ship. At that point, the cycle has become toxic, and communication usually disintegrates.

Changing Yourself

Focusing on changing yourself instead of trying to change others is one of the foundational principles of relationship therapy. Marriage therapists know that one of the most common attributes of troubled marriages is the power struggle that evolves because one or both of the couple is trying to change the other.

Honestly, changing yourself may really be about simply accepting your life for what it is and accepting the limitations we all must endure. But women are bombarded by messages from the media that we can be "all we are meant to be." This vague promise, coming from the potentiality movement, is sometimes just a call to chase an illusion and keeps us from appreciating who we already are and what we already have. Instead of practicing gratitude and thankfulness for what we have, we indulge in wishful thinking and experience a nagging restlessness and dissatisfaction with what may be a perfectly good life. Only you can decide whether that restlessness is a call to make real and positive change or an unrealistic yearning for a life that is not your real path.

Identifying Your Expectations

Everyone goes into relationships with expectations, most of them unspoken. We don't realize the importance of thinking and talking about what we *truly expect* from men *before* we get too involved with them. But considering your expectations and desires for a man—whether realistic *or* unrealistic—will help you know whether you're moving in the right direction with him. Do you expect him to be the sole breadwinner? A great lover? An excellent chef? All of these wishes are understandable, but what if your man can't or won't cook?

Thinking through expectations will help in any relationship, whether you are married now or planning to marry in the future. If you are divorced, it will help you understand what might have gone wrong in the past and how to avoid the same trap with a new man.

What do you expect from your man? Which of your expectations are fair, and which are over the top? What are the "deal breakers" in this relationship; the things you cannot live without? There is no question that working through these questions will not only improve communication, it will improve you. Because instead of trying to change him, you will begin to accept and truly love him *for him*. Of course, you will also realize just how arrogant us women can be.

Our desires to change our men are really very narcissistic. By narcissism, I mean that we want the man we love to reflect *our* tastes, *our* views, and *our* lifestyle choices. We make it all about us! Ironically, when we first become involved with someone we are really attracted to, we often do the exact opposite: we *accommodate* the man. We present ourselves as someone we aren't and pretend we enjoy things we don't just to convince him we are a good match for him. We don't admit to ourselves that we are putting up a false front to please him or that we have a hidden agenda to change him once we've snagged him. We convince ourselves that he will be so happy and so fulfilled once he is with us, he won't mind. It is only after we are in a committed relationship with him

> *It's crucial to determine and share your expectations in order to know just how compatible you and your man are and whether you both view expectations in the same light.*

that we allow the masks to come down and the issues we dislike to surface, and that is when your man is very likely to accuse you of "not being the woman he married" or having been dishonest with him when you were dating. Those are character traits you *can* work on changing about yourself—and you should, because they're certainly not flattering. Becoming less self-focused will make it easier for you to find the good in others instead of zeroing in on the flaws you want to change.

Changing a Toad

Of course, there are true toads—men whose behaviors and attitudes are crude, lacking in character, common sense, goodness, or sensitivity (quite different from the frogs we talked about earlier). Toads aren't always bad men, but they aren't exactly good men, either.

Unfortunately, there are many women who are attracted to men like this, for several different reasons. Toads can be very entertaining, and some are occasionally fun. In fact, there is a good chance that a woman and her toad may have a rather intense chemical attraction going on, especially if she dallies in the swamp a bit too long.

But a swamp is no place for girls looking for good men. Yes, these swamp creatures might be cute, but they are still toads, and they can pull you down into the slime when you least expect it.

Many women don't get this. We make the mistake of thinking that it is possible to find good "material"—a work in progress, so to speak—in places most good men don't frequent. We look for our potential mates in all the wrong places (like cheap bars and clubs) and then wonder why they don't quit going to bars and clubs after we marry them. We fall in love with men from extremely troubled families who show all the signs of following the same path, and then wonder why we cannot change them into men who are kind and caring to us.

But once we wake up and realize we're in a swamp, instead of having the courage to admit we've taken the wrong path, we often decide that all we need to do is make the swamp a little more like home. So we set up camp, hang curtains, have babies, and try to pretend we are with the man of our dreams instead of a toad.

> *Marriage only makes men more of what they already are. If they are good men, they will probably get better, and if they are not good, they will only get worse.*

Shannon, even though she was with a good fellow, not a toad, was still in a swamp of her own making. Anyone who is ambivalent about marrying shouldn't do so, no matter how many other people we make unhappy in the process. We should pay attention when we feel uncertain, because it is our intuition and our deep spiritual selves warning us that we are about to make a huge mistake.

Hear this: *You cannot change a man, especially after you marry him.*

I simply cannot make this point strong enough. Women often think marriage will change men. It rarely does; *it only makes them more of what they already are.* If they are good men, they will probably get better, and if they are not good, they will only get worse.

Of course, there are exceptions to every rule, and I'm sure many of you reading this are summoning up stories you know of women who prayed their men into a better place or helped their man change his ways by being patient and kind and forgiving.

That is perfectly fine.

But in those cases, the women were probably already married to them, and they got lucky. Their stories are statistically rare.

As for toads? The best way to avoid them is to stay away from the places where you meet them. But honestly, they are everywhere these days—even in church. So if you cannot avoid them altogether, you are going to have to hone your toad detector, and learn to do a better job of spotting them.

Be especially careful of the man with the sad life story who attempts to convince you that he has managed to survive all of it unscathed, and he only needs for you to teach him how to be a better man. If he is unscathed, he is a better man already and doesn't need you to do that for him. You are not his teacher, and he will resent your efforts to be one once you are married to him. It is not that you should necessarily stay away from all men with horrendous family histories—sometimes that does make a man stronger, and surviving a bad family can create an incredibly good man. What you must do is make sure he is good *before* you marry him.

What if you are already married, and your plans to change your man didn't work? Taking *positive action* (there are those words again) is the only thing that will change your situation, even if it doesn't change the man. For example, learn how to encourage, reward, and reinforce the behaviors you want in your man. This is not manipulative or an attempt to change the *man*; you are simply changing his *behavior*, which is entirely different. Stop being whiny and critical of the things you don't like; instead praise and give positive attention to the things you do like.

Out of the Swamp

To sum it up, two of the reasons women try to change men is that they fail to recognize a prince, or they fail to be satisfied with a perfectly good frog. It is important to realize that many times the two issues are two sides of one coin. The bottom line is that whichever one applies, neither one is very respectful or kind to our man.

Essentially, I'm declaring a "Be Kind to Frogs Day" . . . every day. That means you've got to quit throwing your frog against the wall when you don't get the change you want as quickly as you want it, hoping a prince might be hidden inside. It just isn't fair. You wouldn't want your man to do that to you, so you shouldn't do it to him.

The best way to avoid the trap of trying to change a man is to make sure you are satisfied with your man just the way he is before you take the relationship further. The rule of thumb is to ask yourself "If he never changes, am I satisfied with him now?" *You don't marry potential, you marry the man.* You love who he is, not what you think he might become.

The best way to ensure that you are not expecting too much of someone is to be upfront early in a relationship about what you expect from a relationship. Don't be afraid you are going to scare a man off by telling him what you expect from a husband once your relationship begins to feel serious. But also make absolutely certain that you aren't setting the bar so high that a good man could never make you happy, just because he doesn't come with all the trappings of royalty.

This doesn't mean that you grill a man, hand him a list of your expectations, or make him feel like he is under a microscope. Many women *do* scare off men by making them feel like they are interviewing for a job instead of looking for a relationship.

This chapter's getting romance right rule advises you to change yourself. This means that you are going to have to change your unrealistic expectations, the false belief that you have the right to change someone else, and the tendency to use the men you date as safety nets when you are afraid of life.

If you are married to someone who should change but won't, then you are going to have to make the decision whether or not to stay with him and live with your lot.

Here's what I know for sure: prayer can make a difference. If you haven't tried prayer, you might find it helpful. What's best about prayer is that it usually changes us more than it changes others, and that could be the most satisfying change of all.

*O*nce upon a time there was a little girl who lived on the edge of a dark, dark forest. This little girl often wore a pretty red cape with a hood, and so people called her Little Red Riding Hood.

One morning, Little Red Riding Hood's mother said to her, "Sweetheart, I've packed a basket with some cookies and a pot of soup. Would you take them to your grandmother on the other side of the forest? She's been feeling a little sick."

So Little Red Riding Hood took the basket and started down the path through the forest.

"Don't dawdle," called her mother from the door. "And don't talk to strangers!"

But Little Red Riding Hood forgot her mother's warnings almost immediately. In the forest were some very pretty flowers, and [she] stopped to pick some for her grandmamma. Suddenly in front of her was a great big wolf.

"Hello," said the wolf. "What's a sweet little girl like you doing in the forest?"

— FROM LITTLE RED RIDING HOOD,
TOLD BY THE BROTHERS GRIMM

CHAPTER 8

Rapunzel

A Cautionary Tale about Loneliness

In this folk tale, our fair maiden, Rapunzel, "lets down her hair," climbs down from her tower, and without a second thought goes riding merrily off into the sunset with a man she doesn't know. Now, how smart is that? Apparently, she doesn't think she needs to ask who he is, where he comes from, or anything about his family, character, or goals. Of course, that is exactly what many women do when they are lonely and desperate for companionship—we ride off with the first man who comes along. (By the way, in folklore, hair is a symbol for sexuality, so Rapunzel's actions are just a teensy bit more complicated than they first appear.)

But why did Rapunzel settle for a man who might be totally wrong for her, leaving her more desperate than before? What if she was rescued by someone without any character, or even someone dangerous? And why do we do the same sorts of things with the men we date or the men we marry? I think the answer has its root in loneliness; we are so hungry to just be with someone that we don't give much thought to *who* that someone is . . . which is why we need this next rule:

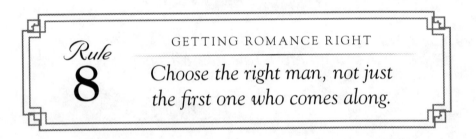

Rule
8

GETTING ROMANCE RIGHT

Choose the right man, not just the first one who comes along.

All of us have to deal with loneliness from time to time—it is a natural part of the human condition. It's like a bad-hair day, a fat day, and an ugly day all in one, and it seems like it just won't end.

But many women suffer a chronic and intense kind of loneliness that leaves them feeling isolated from the rest of the world, like Rapunzel. And that kind of loneliness can creep right into the way we handle our relationships with men.

There are two major destructive influences that this kind of loneliness has on women's relationships with men: (1) we feel we must settle for whomever comes our way because we cannot stand being alone, and (2) we become vulnerable to men who would take advantage of our loneliness for their ulterior and selfish motives. Both are not only stupid, they're unhealthy and potentially dangerous. So it's important to understand why many women become so lonely that it distorts their relationships, how this makes them vulnerable, and how to break that pattern.

Audrey's Story

Audrey was a very successful thirtysomething accountant in a large city in North Carolina. She lived alone in a downtown loft in a trendy area of the business district. As a petite, attractive brunette who made an excellent salary, she was often asked out on dates, primarily by up-and-coming business executives in town. It was not unusual for her to enjoy spa weekends, frequent dinners at the nicest restaurants in town, and several cruises a year. She also was a marathon runner and especially loved kayaking and wilderness hiking. To other women, Audrey appeared to be living a dream life.

But in truth, she was angry, sad, and felt very disconnected from family and friends. She had no close girlfriends, no real interest in spiritual matters, and had not been in a serious relationship for a number of years, although she was far from celibate.

She came to counseling in an effort to deal with her feelings of loneliness. She had achieved the majority of her career and financial goals, and though she did not particularly want children, she was unhappy that she hadn't met a man she wanted to share her life with. Most men she met were already married or seemed threatened by her early success and financial acumen. Several brief affairs had left her unfulfilled.

Audrey's loneliness, and the depression I later diagnosed, stemmed from trauma due to a childhood car accident that killed her mother and left Audrey unharmed. After her father remarried a woman who was not kind to her, Audrey moved across the country and enrolled in a major university in an effort to distance herself from her memories and her family.

During college, Audrey avoided dating and focused on her studies. But once she entered the workforce, her life became punctuated by a series of relationships that she always ended before they required any kind of long-term commitment. With her history of parental abandonment and trauma, she was afraid to trust anyone who claimed to love her, believing in her heart that whoever she loved would come to a tragic end.

She found solace in her academic achievements, career, and disciplined regime of nutrition and fitness, but became lonelier with each passing year. Her father's recent death was her catalyst for seeking help.

As her therapist, I was concerned that Audrey, entrenched in loneliness and fear of commitment, was about to do something terribly rash. She admitted that she'd begun bar hopping by herself or staying up half the night talking to men in chat rooms, who often made attempts to get her to meet them for sex. She claimed it was all a game to her, and she was teasing the men for entertainment. But later Audrey acknowledged that sometimes she wondered how it would be to actually meet one of the men in person. She'd become quite attached to a particular man, even though she confessed she knew very little about him except what he'd told her.

I felt that Audrey's loneliness was driving her into risky, uncommitted sexual behaviors that could be very dangerous, and possibly into the arms of a man who could be misleading her about himself. Think about Rapunzel. Didn't she do the same? After all, she knew nothing about the man who climbed into her tower.

Why So Lonely?

Audrey's loneliness was primarily self-imposed. Women who are intensely lonely often choose to be alone rather than risk commitment with someone. They are more afraid of abandonment than they are of loneliness—until the loneliness gets to them and they run off with the wrong man, of course. But choosing to avoid relationships altogether is an unhealthy way to live life, and it could mean that we become so desperate that we forget to be wise in our selection of men, and we're back to Rapunzel again.

Another kind of loneliness affects some women who have simply never learned how to be *alone* in a productive way. They are not traumatized or grief-stricken; they are simply natural extroverts. Unlike introverts who don't really need people to feel whole and complete, extroverts must have relationships—the more the better—in order to function emotionally and intellectually. Often, the mere thought of being by themselves for more than a few hours makes them uncomfortable. Sometimes it can be so extreme that they can't shake the belief that they've been totally forgotten by everyone when they are alone.

A sense of loneliness can be byproduct of a chemical imbalance in the brain and is one of the traits of those with addictive tendencies. The chemicals related to mood, sleep, and a sense of well-being (like serotonin, endorphins, etc.) also regulate our feelings of connection to others. Food, sex, and drugs are often used to assuage loneliness, because they change brain chemistry. They may temporarily relieve loneliness, but in the long run, using those substances only increases our depression and isolation from others, and we end up more lonely than ever.

Often, the mere thought of being by themselves for more than a few hours makes extroverts uncomfortable.

Some people perpetuate loneliness by simply believing what they see on TV. It can be much easier to stay home and entertain ourselves by watching fictional programs or reality television, and we can start to believe that we are a part of TV characters' lives. What we don't realize is that making a habit of this—which many lonely women do—*increases* the feeling of being chronically isolated from the world. After a while, we can forget how to use our social skills or how to sustain relationships over the long haul.

Television ads consistently send us a message that is totally untrue: *If you are beautiful and loveable, you will never be alone.* But when nothing we buy proves to make us quite beautiful or loveable enough, and we are still alone, we start to believe something is wrong with us. We question whether anyone will *ever* love us. The longer this goes on, the lonelier we become. That is when we "settle" for the first man who comes along.

When Loneliness Makes You Settle

One of the more subtle, and socially acceptable, *stupid* mistakes is to settle for someone just because we are afraid of being alone. The fear of being alone can push women—whatever their age—into relationships that otherwise they'd never dream of forming. They settle for any number of men who aren't right for them: married men, men with whom they have absolutely nothing in common, or men who have bad habits that the lonely women overlook. Many women would rather have someone than no one at all, so they settle for less. It's important to note, however, that settling isn't always about scraping the bottom of the barrel. It can be about not choosing the best person but taking what comes our way.

Of course, settling is not the same as choosing an imperfect man. Nobody is flawless, and no man is going to suit you *perfectly* in every way you desire or expect. Just like we learned from the princess and her frog, trying to fit a man into a mold we determine will get us nowhere.

> *Settling is not the same as choosing an imperfect man. Nobody is flawless, and no man is going to suit you perfectly in every way you desire or expect.*

But choosing someone who *clearly* isn't right for us, or worse, someone who has a laundry list of bad habits, just to escape our loneliness rarely brings peace and fulfillment. Once we make a commitment to that person, we frequently deal with an ongoing sense of uneasiness about him. And we often question whether we've made the right decision—especially when deficiencies or dysfunctions in our relationship begin to emerge. We may find ourselves with someone with whom we feel very little intimacy or deep connection, which may lead to a greater loneliness than ever.

There has been a rise in the number of single, divorced, and widowed women in the United States today. Women over the age of forty who are living alone outnumber men almost eleven to one. This kind of statistic haunts many women, who become fearful that their chances of marrying or remarrying are dwindling with each passing year. And settling out of loneliness can seduce us into accepting behaviors and attitudes that we shouldn't have to tolerate, much less live with.

This is where the wolves, snakes, and lost boys come in. It's a sad truth that there are plenty of men out there who *intend* to take advantage of women, lonely women in particular. And this may come as a surprise, but it is often women of faith who are the most trusting. They've been praying for a good husband, and lo and behold, a new man shows up at church just when they had almost given up on finding a mate for life.

It is a harsh reality, but the truth is that women still need protection from wolves, snakes, and lost boys, whether we've lived sheltered lives or are relatively sophisticated and liberal.

Protecting Ourselves

It used to be that when a woman met a man, the first thing she did was bring him home to meet her parents, no matter her age. Now that is considered to be horribly old-fashioned and the theme of dark comedies and spoofs on terrible in-laws. Often we deliberately exclude the people in our lives who might be able to see what we would rather *not* see and who encourage us to be accountable for our choices.

I'm not advocating a return to the time when women had to ask permission from their parents to marry. But we can be so eager to prove how mature we are that we push aside our parents, never encouraging a positive relationship between our mate and family. That doesn't lay a great foundation for your marriage. Involving your parents and extended family during your courtship can be a protective factor. Aunts, cousins, brothers, and mamas seem to have built-in toad detectors!

Those couples who choose a wedding ceremony that symbolizes their commitment to each other, and preferably to God, and that announces to the world that each person in a couple is *who they say they are*, stand a greater chance of their marriage working. It doesn't matter whether the ceremony happens in a church, in a city hall, or on a beach somewhere, there needs to be full disclosure, family involvement, and a sense of how serious the vows really are.

But today's girls typically get engaged and married, and all their parents do is pay the bills and show up to give away the bride, with little involvement in the process. Often the people who love her—family, friends, coworkers, etc.—don't know anything about her man, other than that she is marrying him.

It may seem tacky, but you need to make sure your man doesn't have a criminal history, is not a sex offender, or have a lousy credit score. Those three things are indicators of major problems that could haunt you for the rest of your life. You also need to pay attention to the serious hereditary disorders in his family, especially mental illness. That doesn't mean you shouldn't marry him; it simply means that you should be aware of what you might face in the future.

Lonely Women and Married Men

One pattern I've noticed in counseling women is that when they are lonely, many tend to be attracted to married men. In fact, there are just as many lonely married women as there are lonely single women. Either group is at risk for extramarital affairs, which can lead to terrible problems in both our personal and professional lives.

For women who are married and lonely, it sometimes feels easier to build an exciting, intimate relationship with someone new rather than to work hard to rebuild intimacy with a spouse. This is especially true if he isn't sensitive or doesn't seem to care that we are lonely. It may seem easier to talk with someone we don't have a painful history with.

That is a trap straight from the pit of hell.

The truth is, when relationships begin as acts of betrayal, regardless of how "right" they may seem, how rational their reasons, or how good they feel, they are doomed to failure—to the tune of about 80 to 90 percent.

It should go without saying that it's best to avoid married men altogether. Some of these men are looking for sex because they are bored with their wives, and another woman seems to make them feel better about themselves. But often these men are suffering the same kind of loneliness we are. Regardless of the reason, being lonely doesn't give anyone license to jump into an adulterous relationship. It will not only hurt you—yes, it will make you even lonelier in the long run—but it also hurts the man and those in his life to whom he has pledged his love.

> *When relationships begin as acts of betrayal, they are doomed to failure— to the tune of about 80 to 90 percent.*

Our Own Best Friend

It may sound clichéd, but solitude really is good for the soul, if it is cultivated for the gift that it often is. Many of us don't like being alone because when we are alone we think too much, and usually what we think about is our problems, fears, and failures. We think about ourselves, and most of our thoughts dwell on the negative aspects of our lives.

And I know how it feels when a Sunday afternoon seems to stretch into eternity, when the sound of our thoughts, a ticking clock, or a fly on the windowpane—or rather, the drone of the television—seem to be the only sounds in the entire universe. I think that is why many of us dread getting old: we are afraid that means we might have to be alone.

In our fear, we frantically attempt to distract ourselves by throwing ourselves at a man we hope will free us, not realizing that we will never have a healthy relationship if we don't first learn to be our own best friend.

> *We frantically look for a man we hope will free us from ourselves, not realizing that we will never have a healthy relationship if we don't first learn to be our own best friend.*

We do this first by making friends with God and allowing him to forgive us and show us the amazing things in us that are unique to us. Then we move forward by forgiving ourselves, getting to know ourselves better, and developing passions and interests, apart from romance, that help us learn to like ourselves better.

Seeking Solace and Solutions

Solutions to loneliness come when you stop waiting for someone to take it away and climb down from that tower all by yourself. You do this by changing how you feel about yourself now. That will help ease your loneliness, which will ultimately result in your being less vulnerable to those who would take advantage of you. But it won't happen overnight, and some changes may be hard—especially if you are suffering from depression, financial difficulty, grief, or trauma. But your life may depend on it.

Writing it all down will help. This isn't necessarily journaling, although journaling is therapeutic for just about every problem. I'm talking about writing stories, essays, or even your life history. Many good writers are birthed out of the pain of loneliness and grief, and the world may need what you, too, have to say, whether you write about your experiences, those of others, or make up stories for yourself.

If you cannot write, try painting. Many folk artists with no formal instruction whatsoever in the arts create paintings full of rich meaning and story. It doesn't matter how well you paint, just how much you use your imagination.

How about joining a club that helps you develop a skill? Some of the best ways to meet people is through team sports, such as tournament fishing, softball, or volleyball. Or you can volunteer to work with kids who are lonely and need a mentor or role model. You might meet a man who has similar values as you.

But it is not just about meeting men. It is about forming friendships and emotional connections with all kinds of people, so that your life is rich and full. Making the effort to form emotional connections *before* we become lonely is the key to preventing depression from developing.

If you want good things to happen, you have to expect them. Granted, this is difficult if you feel nothing good has ever happened to you, but that is one of the main reasons you should seek counseling if you are feeling deeply lonely. And your feelings that nothing good has happened should be the major focus of your therapy—because most of us have experienced happiness and blessing, but we've just let the bad things overshadow the good. We sabotage the possibility of good things by focusing too much on our fear and our failures.

A life of hope can take you from being controlled by your hurts to living above them.

If you want to move beyond intense loneliness, you absolutely must try to begin each day with gratitude for what you *do* have— even if by others' standards, your life is very difficult. You might even be disabled, filing for bankruptcy, ill, or heartbroken, but a life of hope can take you from being controlled by your hurts to living above them.

And this is where God comes in. Talk to him honestly about your hurts *and* your hopes. He is listening and he knows how lonely you are. It's true that God loves you and wants you to have the very best life you can. He forgives you when you ask.

If you don't believe in God, that may actually contribute to your loneliness. It is hard to feel connected to the world if you don't believe you are in the world for a reason. The only thing I can do here is petition for your reconsideration. If you actively seek out God and risk believing in something other than yourself, you might just be set free from your high tower. In fact, if there is any magic fairy dust to be had in this world, hope in God is it.

CHAPTER 9

Little Red Riding Hood

Staying Away from Wolves

Oh my, yes. What *was* that sweet little thing doing in the forest, skipping through a dangerous patch of woods all by herself? And why did her mother send her—alone—to her grandmother's house, knowing she had to go through the dark forest to get there? Mothers are supposed to know better.

Of course, there are plenty of girls who take off *without* their mother's permission. After all, big bad wolves *can* be sooooooo exciting, sexy, and handsome. . . .

And *that's* what this chapter is about: women who are attracted to volatile, dangerous men—those big, bad wolves and all the other dangerous creatures who lurk in the forest with them.

Many women don't know why they're so drawn to bad boys or how to change that about themselves, or even how to recognize the obvious warning signs that they are already in the dark forest. To begin the discussion, let's start with a rule to go by:

Rule 9

GETTING ROMANCE RIGHT

Steer clear of the bad boys.

The tale of Little Red Riding Hood is one of those stories we've always heard but never given much thought. Of course, it evolved as a way for mothers to teach their daughters about the dangers of getting romantically involved with the wrong men. After all, the symbols are not difficult to decode. Red is a classic symbol of both sexuality and evil, the path is about the life journey, and the wolf is a sexual predator. Grandma's house is representative of stability, safety, and security.

So Little Red dallies in the forest too long and finds herself staring into the eyes of the wolf. *Surprise, surprise.* Hard to believe she didn't know there might be wolves hanging around. Was she really *that* innocent?

Instead of running, like the SAM she is, she stops and talks to him; and while she continues to pick flowers, he runs to Grandma's house, eats the old woman, and dons her clothing, all in an elaborate game to fool Little Red Riding Hood.

And Little Miss Hood? When she gets to Grandma's house, she recognizes that something is wrong but doesn't follow her instincts. When the wolf pats the bed and coyly suggests she climb aboard, she jumps right in, asking rather stupid questions about the size of certain body parts. Remember: "Oh, what a big nose you have!" Mmmmmmmm. So much for "hidden" symbols. Could it be more obvious?

In my eyes, the story is undoubtedly a sexual cautionary tale and suggests that dangerous men can be found anywhere. Even the homes of trusted loved ones, as the grandma's role implies, are not exempt from leering wolves.

For Stephanie, whose story follows, not only did the wolf find her in the forest but she took him home with her and let him into her heart.

Stephanie's Story

Stephanie, the youngest daughter of a solid, respectable family, came to my office seeking advice about her impending marriage to a man named Eric.

She was beginning to doubt whether she really loved him and worried about what kind of father he might become once they married and had children. She and Eric had dated off and on throughout college and had a history of rather intense arguments that sometimes ended in a breakup. But Eric would always return to her, contrite and begging her forgiveness. Stephanie loved him a great deal and missed him when they were apart.

For the last year, their relationship had seemed to be on an even keel, and now that he had graduated and had a good job, his jealousy and temper tantrums seemed to be a thing of the past. Stephanie reckoned that he'd just needed time to grow up, and it finally seemed he had. The wedding was planned for the summer.

But Stephanie, a rather quiet, shy woman, began to notice things that troubled her after they became engaged. Though somewhat different than in the past, Eric's behaviors seemed to be reemerging. He was the perfect gentleman around her family, but rather mean-spirited and sometimes even cruel to her in front of their friends.

If Stephanie challenged his behavior, he would become cold and distant, and she would later notice him flirting with other women, particularly when he was drinking. He would say cruel things, then tell her "I'm only joking . . ." and accuse her of being too uptight and serious when she complained about his insults. On one occasion, he had grabbed her arm and shoved her against a wall during an argument.

But she loved him and couldn't imagine her life without him. She knew he desperately wanted to marry her, though she questioned if she could spend her life with someone who could be so unkind, and even cruel. On the other hand she felt sorry for him, too. He'd had a rough life, and she felt that she was the only one who truly understood him.

Stephanie told me that she came to counseling hoping to be told that she was just getting cold feet. She was hoping to hear that once they were married, he would change for the better, especially once they had children of their own. (*There's that "change him" idea again.*)

But after a few sessions, there was no way I could confirm her cold-feet theory. There was much more going on. While talking about her childhood, Stephanie shared that during one summer when she was six years old, an older cousin in his teens, whom she idolized, had "played games" with her, insisting that she touch him inappropriately. This happened on several occasions over the summer, but once school started, the family visits stopped, and so did the abuse. But the shame, fear, and confusion of it all had haunted Stephanie, especially because she had never told anyone.

Stephanie also revealed that on and off through high school she had been drawn to the "bad boy," and on one occasion had suffered a nonviolent date rape.

Ongoing sessions helped Stephanie understand her pattern and attraction to abusive men. She slowly began to understand that her feelings of guilt over being molested were normal, but that she had done nothing wrong.

She was also able to see that the molestation had begun in her a pattern of passive acceptance of mistreatment from men. Realizing that her reluctance to marry was based on a fear of continued abuse from Eric, she broke off her engagement and continued counseling. Eric is coming in for counseling with her and has agreed to complete treatment if Stephanie will continue to support him during that process. No decision about a future life together is pending at this time.

Why We Choose the Bad Boys

Stephanie's story tells of the most heartbreaking reason women put up with abusive men: the painful and frightening things that happen to us in our growth years. As with most children who are molested, she was both repulsed and excited by the attention from her older cousin. Those two equally strong and opposing emotions were indelibly stamped on her mind and colored all of her relationships with men from then on.

Counseling reassured Stephanie that her feelings were normal to children, especially her enjoyment of the touching. After all, we are designed to enjoy physical touch.

But this combination of fear, excitement, and pleasurable sensation laid down a neural pathway in her brain that predisposed her to dangerous encounters with men who either took advantage of her or made her feel bad about herself—all of which seemed very normal for her, almost comfortable.

Her worst fear was that she attracted this kind of male because there was something morally wrong with her, and that whatever that was, it made it acceptable for the opposite sex to treat her badly. She blamed herself for having been raped while in high school by an older boyfriend.

She had difficulty understanding when I tried to explain that her date rape should have been reported. She insisted that she'd "led the boy on" or had put herself in harm's way. She also admitted she felt horrible afterward and very ashamed of herself.

I made it clear to her that anytime a man forces sex on a girl, even if it is nonviolent, and even if they are in a situation where the man believes sex is going to happen, it is the woman's right to say no. There is even a law that says so. Ironically, this situation and others like it had only fueled Stephanie's attraction to aggressive men. She just believed that's how men were.

Attraction to dangerous men isn't always about our pasts. More common forms of emotional baggage—many that we've covered in this book—can also lead us to men who would hurt or take advantage of us. We can be like Rapunzel (we'll meet her in the next chapter), who, when lonely and desperate, might have settled for an abusive man if he kept her warm at night. And who knows, Cinderella might be willing to put up with put-downs because her prince has a lot of money and can provide the financial security she desires. Wendy, with her mothering instinct, would probably feel sorry for him and forgive him because he needs *someone* to care for him. And sometimes, it is just the Little Red Riding Hood in us who is stupid enough to dally in the forest and flirt with wolves because we enjoy taking risks.

But there are other dangerous creatures, in addition to aggressive, violent men, who hang out in the dark forest and swamps.

While the wolf is the aggressive, angry, violent man, the snake is a manipulator, someone who intentionally takes advantage of our loneliness or shame, and not only steals our hearts, but often our money, purity, or other things that are precious to us. He is often quite gentlemanly, unlike the wolf or the toad, and he whispers sweet nothings in our ears. He wraps himself around us, and before we know it we are in bed with a married man, forging a check for him, or helping him buy drugs. He never hits us, but he surely breaks our heart. He often ends up in jail, and unfortunately, Little Red often goes down with him.

Why We Fall for Snakes and Wolves

Simply put, girls who take a walk on the wild side and choose the bad boys are usually the girls who, on some level, believe they deserve negative treatment, or don't think they can get a nice guy because they aren't attractive, rich, or smart enough. They may also be hiding secrets of which they are ashamed.

This all contributes to the development of emotional patterns in women—patterns that make them most comfortable when in dangerous, abusive, or simply difficult relationships. Anything that shamed us in the past has the power to make us believe we don't deserve to be treated well in the present.

But there is a catch, and it contributes to why girls with hardly any baggage sometimes get involved with bad boys. To put it bluntly, romance with guys like this can be terribly exciting, and the sex is often incredibly intense. Wolves are oh so good at ringing the little bells in our hearts, and snakes mesmerize us with their charm. It feels so grown up and rebellious to hop in a car (or truck) or on a motorcycle with one of these guys (like in the movies) and leave everyone in a trail of bad-boy dust.

> *Anything that shamed us in the past has the power to make us believe we don't deserve to be treated well in the present.*

The lure of the bad boy is powerful, because he promises experiences and adventures we'd never have in our boring, everyday lives, especially if we have been rather sheltered or we don't think we are attractive enough for a prince. Sometimes it is to prove that we can tame them, in spite of what people say—after all, we believe a good woman is all they need, and we think we've got what it takes to domesticate them. But although wolves and snakes can be exciting, there is nothing smart about getting involved with one; and trust me, they rarely make good house pets.

How to Stay Away from Bad Boys

This part isn't easy. Bad boys are the subject of movies, television, and lots of books (especially romance novels with covers featuring a brawny, shirtless, muscle-laden guy and a buxom female with her cleavage in full array). We get the message constantly that there is something terribly romantic and exciting about the "swarthy stranger" or the bad boys we see in the movies who get the girl in the end. Instead of being a bad man, he turns out to have a good man inside who just needed the love of a woman to bring it out, or he just needed someone to tame him. That is an extremely dangerous myth.

And like all of the fairy tales, we are misled about the eventual outcomes of those heart-pumping trysts, because we are never told how difficult a life with them will be—because for the most part, they are mentally ill.

That's the thing you have to remember. Bad boys are typically mentally unbalanced. They have major personality disorders or chemical or neurological imbalances in their brains that make them dangerous. There is nothing romantic or sexy about that. Sad, but not really sexy.

Of course, it doesn't feel sad at first, and that is why you must try to stay away from them to start with, as hard as that seems at the time. Because—I hate to use this word again—they are addic-tive. They do create the "rush" and the chemical squirts in your brain that will make you as high as Mary Poppins on crack.

> *The thing about bad boys is that they are typically mentally unbalanced. There is nothing romantic or sexy about that.*

And after you've been with a bad boy, nice boys might seem dull and boring, just like life is when you are recovering from any drug. When you've expe-rienced it, anything else after seems bland and tasteless. That is what the snake did for Eve in the Garden of Eden. She took the forbidden fruit . . . and look what happened to her. She ended up in the wilderness.

Snakes and wolves are not creatures to mess with, so keep your distance. But in order to stay away from them, you've got to be able to spot them first.

Looking Out for Wolves and Snakes

Most bad boys are dishonest in general, and their motives are varied, but some also have subconscious issues that they aren't even aware of. Regardless, there are warning signs that you should heed.

Following is a basic list of wolf and snake characteristics, which is not exclusive by any means. Not every man with these characteristics will financially swindle you, romantically dupe you, or physically victimize you. And of course, most wolves and snakes are *not* serial killers, but you still need to be cautious. Don't lower your standards and accept unacceptable behavior just because the guy is cute, funny, rich, or handsome. He is still a snake or a wolf, and both are very dangerous. I promise you, there is no good guy hiding inside waiting for you to free him. A lot of men have these characteristics, and, of course, there are degrees of severity.

Characteristics of a Bad Boy

+ He can explain away almost anything and is usually a sly charmer.

+ He has unexplained money, absences, trips out of town, and telephone calls.

+ He seems hyperalert and overly suspicious of everyone; he may even accuse you of dishonesty, theft, or infidelity.

+ He may be attracted to perverted sex, cult religions, the occult, etc.

+ He assumes the checkbook early in the relationship and may even insist on giving you an "allowance," even if you earned the money.

+ He always has big plans and schemes that require you to invest financially.

- He claims to have no living family or is estranged from them.

- He is excessively vague about his education, work, or military history.

- He wants everything to be put in his name upon marriage.

- One of his favorite lines is "Don't you trust me?"

- When caught red-handed, he seems to have no remorse.

- His friends seem "sleazy."

- He blames others for his problems and convinces you that it is your behavior that pushes him over the edge.

- He often drinks heavily or uses drugs to calm himself down.

- He is controlling, jealous, and wants to isolate you from your family.

- He seems to side with the "bad guy" when watching television or movies.

- He starts a number of jobs and then gets fired or quits because of his temper.

- He avoids serious discussions by initiating sex.

- He hits, shoves, slaps, pulls your hair, and kicks you (even once is not okay).

- He is verbally abusive and tells you that you are fat, stupid, or crazy.

- He is fascinated with weapons.

♦ He likes rough sex and rarely takes no for an answer when he makes sexual advances (history of "date rape"— a nonviolent rape that is still illegal).

When Things Become Dangerous

The above list covers a wide range of characteristics that should suggest a dysfunctional man. But there are times when a man can be more than ill suited for you; he can be dangerous.

When a man calls you names or tells you that you are fat, ugly, or frigid—anything that puts you down and makes you feel bad about yourself no matter what the situation—he is being abusive. If he says mean things about you and your family that you know are not true, that is abusive as well. And if he touches you in any way but gently—you get the picture—he is abusive and danger-ous. Many women try to pretend that these behaviors are not abusive, but rather "forgivable overreactions." But I refuse to let you pretend that's true. You and I both know it: if your man hurts you emotionally or physically, there's no way to pretend.

And if he does any of those things to your children, that is to-tally unacceptable and illegal. You could lose your children if you don't protect them.

Experts used to believe that there was a natural progression of violent behavior that began with verbal abuse then moved to pushing, shoving, cursing, and maybe an occasional slap. Then it notched to a higher level with blows to the head, punches, and knocking down a woman. With no intervention, a violent eruption could then occur that would lead to severe injury or death.

Not so now. Statistics are showing that, in many cases, there may be no period of escalation. Many homicides occur where there is actually very little history of prior violence, except perhaps for minor incidences. Read the list of characteristics carefully, as they are your warning signs that a man has the *potential* to hurt you, even if he hasn't yet.

> *The reality is that a wolf is a wolf. The only thing you can do is stay away from him, even if it is enticing to hang out in the forest with him for a while.*

The violent nature of our society has escalated, as has the addiction to sex, drama, and the worship of romantic love. We see endless stories on television, both real and make-believe, that graphically depict all manner of violence, especially toward women. These depictions often romanticize and distort abuse, planting seeds in their observers. The best thing you can do for yourself is be *honest* and make only decisions that keep you safe and happy.

The reality is that a wolf is a wolf, no matter how sad his life story or what terrible things have happened to him. The only thing you can do is stay away from him, even if it is enticing to hang out in the forest with him for a while.

Only God can tame wolves, and trust me, he would never send them into your life, no matter how pitiful or hungry they might appear. You certainly shouldn't feed or pet them either, not matter how cute and cuddly they may seem.

The Honeymoon Cycle

The "honeymoon cycle" is usually an integral part of the pattern in abusive relationships. It can apply to both emotional and
physical abuse, but is characterized by intense periods of conflict,
followed by a calm period of equally intense romance. In life, the
cycle looks like this:

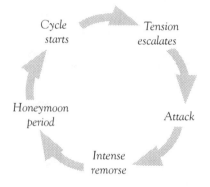

Tension and conflict begin to mount. Violence erupts. Typically, the abuser is contrite and begs for forgiveness. The couple
reconciles, reunites, and there is an intense period of romantic
bliss. For a time, possibly even months, the relationship is wonderful and often becomes incredibly emotional and sexual. In his
guilt, the abuser buys gifts, lavishes attention, and becomes com-
pletely submissive. He begs to be forgiven.

Believe it or not, many women have told me through the
years that they would actually say and do things they knew would
trigger a violent episode. Why? They felt they had no control
over the process, and they wanted to get the violence done with,
so they could move on to the "good times."

Some of my clients have even admitted that it made them feel powerful to be able to make a man lose control. That's Tinker Bell talk for sure. But others simply put up with the cycle because they say they cannot imagine their lives without the sound of his voice, the smell of his skin, or the feel of his touch.

True love does not hurt. On the contrary, it should be a comfort, a source of support, and a soft place to land when you are tired and weary. A couple who truly loves each other experiences much less melodrama—their relationship can sometimes even be "boring." There will be fewer explosive moments. There will be fewer breakups and reunions. And there will certainly be no violence.

But that boringness—or rather, contentment—can be just where happiness lives.

Getting the Help You Need

If you are in a dangerous relationship and you've tried everything you can to improve the situation, please get professional counseling. A good therapist or a counselor at a women's shelter or domestic violence program can teach you how to extricate yourself safely and without violence. Most such organizations have officers on staff who are specially trained in conflict resolution and domestic violence. They understand that when a woman tries to leave a man who is violent or abusive, she is in danger, so they treat her with utmost care.

Unfortunately, I believe many churches or volunteer counselors are not equipped to deal with the problem. In fact, you may have already experienced a pastor telling you that you must stay with a man you've married because you made a vow before God. I can honestly say to you that spiritual directors like this are misguided.

If you are in a violent relationship, get out if you can. If you are in an emotionally abusive relationship, see the list of resources in the back that will help you to recognize and manage emotionally destructive relationships and end them as well. There are wonderful resources out there. I've provided addresses and telephone numbers in the back of this book; call them. Look in the Yellow Pages of your phone book or call 911.

Don't fall into the pity trap either, and don't be foolish enough to believe that the power of your love and prayer will change him. Prayer does have changing power, but only if the person *wants* to change. Many violent men will try to convince you that you are responsible for their problems and that you have the power to destroy them emotionally if you leave. Ironically, it is sometimes your leaving that forces him to get the help he needs.

If a man is sincere about changing, the proof will be in the doing. He will go to classes (without always being court-ordered), he will seek professional help, and he will follow through on what he learns. Never accept promises, tears, vows to change, or a few trips to church as proof of change.

Ditch the cape and stay out of the woods, Little Red. Take another path to Grandma's house.

*O*ne day a young man came riding through the forest. He heard the witch call to Rapunzel, saw Rapunzel lean out the window, and he fell in love with her in a moment.

So he waited for the witch to go away again, and when she had gone, he went to the foot of the tower and called out, "Rapunzel! Let down your hair!"

Rapunzel thought it was the witch calling, so she was shocked when the young man climbed in at her window instead. She had never seen any other person besides the witch, and she marveled at the stranger who now stood in her room. But the man spoke kindly to her of the wide world that she had never known, so when he asked her to come away with him, she answered, "Yes!"

— FROM RAPUNZEL, IN *TALES FROM THE BROTHERS GRIMM,* COMPILED BY COOPER EDEN

PART IV

Into the Light

*I*f human beings are not drowned," asked the little mermaid, "can they live forever? Do they never die as we do here in the sea?"

"Yes," replied the old lady, "they must also die, and their term of life is even shorter than ours . . . [but] they have a soul which lives forever, lives after the body has been turned to dust. It rises up through the clear, pure air beyond the glittering stars." . . .

"Why have not we an immortal soul?" asked the little mermaid mournfully. "I would give gladly all the hundreds of years that I have to live, to be a human being only for one day, and to have the hope of knowing the happiness of that glorious world above the stars."

—FROM A COPY OF THE ORIGINAL MANUSCRIPT OF
THE LITTLE MERMAID, WRITTEN BY HANS CHRISTIAN ANDERSEN, 1836

CHAPTER 10

The Little Mermaid

The Girl Who Got It Right

Okay, dear reader, you've finally made it though the dark forest and taken a journey through some pretty difficult chapters. You should be proud of yourself. That journey might not have been easy for you, but now you are ready to walk into the light of a brand-new day.

But as the Little Mermaid knew, even with all the stuff we humans must face and the stupid mistakes we make, life is still wonderful. She understood that to be human is to be fully alive, to have a soul.

When I was studying the different fairy tales featured in this book, I was frustrated because, as you know by now, almost all of them end up with the girl being rescued by the prince, in spite of the odds. And because most of them were written in a time when women were taught not to take matters into their own hands, the women in the stories all waited quietly for their rescue—passive victims of poison, evil witches, lying fathers, or neglectful mothers.

My dilemma was in finding a story that had a heroine who was smart, and yet all of them seemed pretty stupid to me.

Then I stumbled upon the original version of *The Little Mermaid*, written in 1823. I'd always thought about the Disney version, which is a sweet story. But again, it pointed to *romance* as the reason the young mermaid would give up her life in the water, become human, and of course . . . live happily ever after. But the original version showed a much deeper, richer tale.

The Little Mermaid is the youngest of King Neptune's seven daughters, each allowed, on her sixteenth birthday, to rise up out of the water for one day in order to see the world before returning home to live beneath the sea forever.

After hearing the accounts of her sisters and their wonder and awe at all the ships, cities, and beautiful things in the world, it is finally the Little Mermaid's turn. But once on the earth, she is in awe—not of the material things, but of the beauty of the stars and sky and the wonder of what might lie beyond. Then, unexpectedly, her life is changed forever when she saves the prince from drowning and experiences her first brush with death. Much to her dismay, this leads to her discovery that mermaids, unlike humans, do not have a soul.

According to legend, mermaids lived for hundreds of years,

but had no soul or connection to God through spirit. Only humans get to go to heaven. The Little Mermaid was smart because she realized that she couldn't be happy without that connection to God and the hope of an afterlife. After all, what meaning does life have if all we do is simply exist for a while and then are gone for eternity, as if who we are, what we do, and the legacy we leave behind don't matter.

When I read this, I almost fell out of my chair. Now *that* girl is smart. The story summed up exactly the message that underscores this entire book: happiness is not about getting a man; it is about finding your soul. If you do that, then everything else will fall into place.

> *Happiness is not about getting a man; it is about finding your soul. If you do that, then everything else will fall into place.*

And isn't it wonderful that her prince becomes her true love, not because she is a victim, but because she is a powerful creature willing to risk her own life to save another, without any romantic motive at all? *Yes!*

Just as the Little Mermaid realized, you are not simply breathing, eating, and plodding through another day for no good reason. *Oh no.* And unlike the Little Mermaid, you are fortunate enough to already be human, to have a soul, and that is a wonderful gift, in spite of your lot down here on earth. If you have a soul, then anything is possible, especially if you are hoping, praying, and holding on to your faith. That means you are growing, and that means you are well on your way to getting smart about men!

Working Our Way Toward Smart

Some of you may have made a few wrong turns, but you can always get back on the path and turn in the right direction. This time, I hope you won't stop and talk to any old wolves, either. And so I am here to tell you the good news: *You are going to be just fine.*

Yeah, I'm talking to *you*, friend, and I'm not trying to give you false hope. You *are* going to be okay, if that is what you truly want. In spite of all the dire warnings and sad stories, the good news here is that being stupid is a treatable condition, and if you pay attention to directions and swallow the medicine, then you should be well on your way to getting romance right.

How do I know? Because you were smart enough to read a book meant to help, and if you are that smart, then you have what it takes to make your life better. Recognizing the need for help is always the first step toward any kind of recovery, and being stupid about men is something *every* woman wants to—and can—get over.

If I thought you couldn't have true, healthy love in your life, overcome your past, and get at least some of that happily-ever-after, I wouldn't bother to even write this chapter. But because I really do believe you can have wonderful romantic relationships, I'm going to tell you just how to get them. This chapter will show you how to spot a true prince and how to make sure you are ready for him when he comes. Though it's not up to you to decide when or if he comes; but you do get to decide to live a full and happy life, with or without a man—and when he does arrive, he'll find that very attractive.

So let's talk about the kind of man worthy of your time, life, and love.

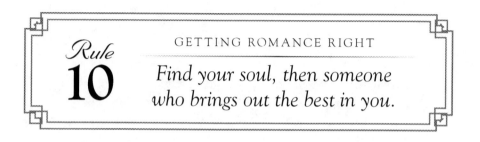

Rule
10

GETTING ROMANCE RIGHT

Find your soul, then someone who brings out the best in you.

Ironically, if you stop and think about it, this rule just about sums it all up. It touches on everything we've discussed, because the foundational principle for successful human relationships, particularly romantic ones, is choosing someone who works at being unselfish and kind—and someone who inspires you to be unselfish and kind as well. And so I give you "the big five," a list for spotting a good man—a man who brings out the best in you.

The Five Cs

So what are we supposed to look for in a man?

No matter the circumstances under which you meet him, these are the five main attributes that you must make priorities if you want a stable relationship. These have to be more important than just about anything. To help you remember them, they all start with the letter C.

But remember that no man is perfect. He should be strong in all five of these areas, but he won't get it right all of the time, and neither will you. If you are a perfectionist, you may look for the one thing in this list that will disqualify any man, and that wouldn't be fair. These are simply guidelines, not rigid rules. The first item on the list is the most important, but after that the characteristics pretty much carry equal weight and are not listed in descending order.

1. Character

Absolutely, he must be of good character with strong moral qualities. Here are some examples of a man of good character: He is honest and dependable when no one is looking, when he doesn't have to be. When he makes a mistake, he owns up to it, and if he does something wrong, he shows true remorse. (Notice that I said that when he makes mistakes, he will own up to them, not that he won't make them.) The difference between a prince and a man who is stupid about women (or life) is that a prince has a history of *learning* from his mistakes. A man of good character is not just sorry because he got caught or temporarily contrite because you are mad at him; he regrets his actions because he knows they were wrong.

A man of character has integrity, is dependable, and can be counted on. He is trustworthy. You can trust him with your children, your money, and your heart because he has a good track record on all those counts. He is gentle and kind.

2. Compatibility

You must be compatible with a man if you are going to share your life with him.

You should have some common interests, shared goals and values, and similar tastes in important things. The same is true in a lesser degree regarding social compatibility, extended family, and issues of financial dependence. We tend to experience the most successful relationships with people like ourselves.

It is especially important for a couple to be equally matched in terms of both intelligence and spiritual values. Those two ingredients are the bedrock of strong relationships.

Although it is human nature to be attracted to our opposites (long story, but attraction of opposites really is biologically based), once we are together, we engage in power struggles with them. That is human, too. Go figure.

A successful relationship with someone who is your opposite is not impossible; it just takes more work. I am married to my opposite, and honestly, our marriage has been very difficult. But we hung in there, and a tremendous amount of goodness has come into our lives as a result.

So if you are already in a relationship with someone who is significantly different from you, your relationship is not doomed. Of course not. But you will have to find ways to work around those differences, compensate for them, and be sensitive to them. It is largely a matter of respecting the other person's differences and finding ways to connect. The trick is learning to step in tune and be considerate of the other's slower or faster pace. It is when the two of you are struggling *against* each other or going in opposite directions that you will likely have difficulties. It all goes back to that kindness and being unselfish principle again. When couples experience problems, it is almost always because one or both of the two is just being selfish.

> *When couples experience problems, it is almost always because one or both of the two is just being selfish.*

Realistically, you do not **need** to find a perfectly matched prince. Sometimes differences can make life more interesting and provide some balance. We don't have to find our twin or someone who magically completes our sentences, just someone who matches us on the most strategic and foundationally important points—like values, life goals, priorities, and matters of faith. The rest is negotiable. He may not like the same music as you, or the same food. You may actually help each other learn to appreciate things you would have otherwise never have enjoyed.

Sometimes differences can challenge us and make us grow, but no one enjoys fighting against another's personality and choices every single day of their lives, not even the Little Mermaid. I've always wondered if she and the prince ever dined on fish. . . .

3. Communication

The ability to communicate with your man is vital. So why do so many couples come to me and tell me they have a "communication problem"? It is because they talk and argue all day, but nothing is being processed. They get nowhere in their conversations, covering the same old ground without any sort of mutual understanding. They don't feel *understood* by the other—and understanding is the essence of communication. When you don't communicate well, you will not understand each other. And it is difficult to love and share good times with someone you don't understand or with someone you won't listen to because you think you have him all figured out.

Being able to communicate well is an art that a good prince (or princess!) knows. Good communication is about listening, being diplomatic, and speaking kindly—not in a condescending, superior, or argumentative manner.

The art of communication is hearing and understanding what another person is saying, validating their feelings about the issue being discussed, and reflecting back to them that you have absorbed their intent and meaning.

That is a radical idea for most couples.

Most communication between arguing couples is two individuals trying to convince the other to see things their way. We've already made up our minds that we are right, so we feel it is our job to convince the other to buy into our viewpoint. We are so busy thinking about the point we want to make, we don't really listen to what the other person has to say. Thus we never learn from each other.

But effective communication is about learning, not just telling our side of things. It is not about winning a debate. If you debate, you won't ever really learn anything from the other person. The key to successful relationships is the ability to listen and validate without turning information-sharing into a verbal power struggle. We need to put on our grown-up pants and take the neutral stance of truly *hearing*.

Listen to your man. *Really* listen, and don't jump in to argue with him. Validate his point of view, even if you don't agree with it. That doesn't mean you've lost anything or that you've given in to him. You are just letting him know that he has a right to his feelings and you to yours, and that you both have valid points. Above all, do what you can to keep discussion neutral; avoid accusation, name-calling, low emotional punches, judgmental statements, and negative body language.

This brings up another important point: *A man cannot read your mind.*

A lot of movies and television programs perpetuate the romantic myth that a man's ability to know what we are thinking and what we need is a natural byproduct of his love and his intimate knowledge of us. We expect men to read our minds, even when we may not know what we are thinking ourselves.

Some women think they are good mind readers themselves, and this leads them to jump to conclusions about what is going on in their man's head, without bothering to discuss it with him. But how can he be open and honest with us if we make him feel we are right about everything?

This is further complicated because women are neurologically wired to be communicators and to verbally process our thoughts out loud; therefore, we can talk circles around men, which confuses even a good man. Our man may be a good communicator, and we won't even know it because we never give him the chance! Of course, there are many of us who are just argumentative and hotheaded by nature. When we argue, we come dangerously close to getting a bad case of diarrhea of the mouth, just because it feels good to vent. We spew out our anger and pain, and in that moment, we don't really care who we hurt. Truth is, this is acid to any relationship and can border on verbal abuse. If this is something you or your man is guilty of, then you need to learn anger management, in addition to better communication skills.

4. Compassion

A real prince has great compassion for all living things, especially you. Compassion simply is more than feeling sorry for someone—it is caring enough to actually try to help others. A prince stoops down to talk to a child, listens to your grandpa's stories, and volunteers his time for good causes.

He is respectful of your feelings and sensitive to your needs. He doesn't treat you like a child, preach at you, or condescend to you. But he doesn't allow you to run over him like a verbal freight train either. He knows how to stand up for himself without retaliating, turning passive-aggressive, or overreacting. He is protective, but not in a jealous, mean-spirited way. There is a big difference.

He may be kind, but he doesn't allow others to take advantage of him, which means he has healthy, strong boundaries.

5. Chemistry

Chemistry is necessary, and I'm talking about a *whole* lot more than sex. A visceral love for and attraction to your man may be the glue that keeps you together even when you don't like each other very much.

You do know that even couples in good marriages don't always like each other, don't you? Women fall in and out of love all the time with their husbands. A smart woman married to a man she knows is fundamentally good learns how to ride out those less-than-amorous spells, waiting for them to pass, instead of filing divorce papers.

That's when chemistry helps the most. Authentic chemistry is a sense of being drawn together in such a way that at the end of the day, when you are bone tired and broke, it is a comfort to crawl into bed together, for more than just sex. Sometimes sex goes away for a while, too. But over time, for people who have true chemistry, it usually comes back around, especially after PMS or hot flashes pass or after depression fades.

But we've made chemistry more important in dating and romance than it needs to be. When love is right, so is the chemistry. It is natural and something you cannot manufacture; and if protected, it usually grows over time. It's the spark of life that attracts others to us because we are healthy and happy—and like any spark, we can fan it into flame or we can douse it with coldness and neglect.

Soul Mates or Spirit Mates?

Long held as the consummate model for relationships, the term *soul mate* is not only overused but also unrealistic and somewhat inaccurate.

Of course, when most people think of soul mates, they think

of people who were "meant to be together," as preordained by God, Jesus, karma, intelligent design, or whatever forces they believe decide our fates.

But many a SAM woman believed she found that soul mate, so she married him and had his babies. After a while, she wonders what in the world happened to that deep sense of connection, familiarity, and "meant-for-each-other" feeling that surged through her veins when they first met. She grieves because she thinks it is gone or that it may never have existed at all.

It's very possible to have a soul-mate, or emotional, connection with a man who is all wrong for you. Many extramarital affairs start just like that, and once acted on, people eventually learn the hard way that their feelings misled them down a very difficult path.

The concept of soul mates can be more accurately attributed to a biochemical reaction in the brain that creates intense romantic feeling, instead of an actual metaphysical epiphany. Instead of a joining of souls, we actually experience an emotional high brought on by increased output of specific chemicals in our brain—chemicals that are designed to make us "see stars." The Little Mermaid saw stars, but they made her think of heaven, not a man.

Those chemicals temporarily draw us together, but they wear off as time goes by; and at that point, we become disillusioned. In other words, the magic fairy dust wears off. This process occurs at an even faster pace if we allow ourselves to become bored or stuck in a rut, or if things happen that destroy our idealistic vision of our partner. When he falls off our finely constructed pedestal, hearts can break.

That doesn't mean you aren't supposed to be together. We sometimes fall off of our mates' pedestals, too, and that can be hard on our bottoms and our hearts. But part of growing up is accepting the fact that we are both human, getting over our unrealistic expectations of each other, and realizing we are all flawed people. That doesn't make our man wrong for us or a bad person. We just both need some attitude adjustments. We need to learn how to really love him, instead of just being "in" love with him.

Instead of *soul mate*, I prefer using the term *spirit mate*. Our spiritual nature is what connects us to God. When we have a relationship with God, our spirit is joined with his. If we are simply soul mates with a man, we are connected in our minds and emotions, but we have no faith or spiritual connection. That leaves out the most important aspect of what we could enjoy with him. Sadly, if you settle for someone with whom you have no spiritual relationship, you are settling for only a small fraction of the beautiful relationship God intended you to have with a man.

Our interactions with a spirit mate will always serve to mold us into better people, more capable of reflecting the qualities of God in our lives, even if the process is painful at times. Our true spirit mate always tries to help us in that process, and we try to help him.

Spirituality in its truest form requires laying down our baggage (our wounds, mistakes, anger, etc.) and learning how to fly, metaphorically speaking. Flying is an ancient symbol in folklore, scripture, and dream interpretation meant to denote spiritual readiness to leave our bodies and soar in the heavens—and home to our Creator.

But instead, we make the mistake of looking for companions who will make life easy and fun. We look for a Peter Pan, or we settle for the earthbound creatures like toads and wolves.

We must find a spiritual man who shares our faith and understands that one of his jobs in life is to help us learn how to fly. And that is one of our jobs, too; we are meant to do more than just run and play with him, keep him happy in bed, and serve him his supper. We are to help him fly. And when one of us breaks a wing, the other is there to mend it and help make it strong again.

That learning process, even when you are with your spirit mate, is sometimes difficult, and may involve financial struggle, moral failures, and head-on collisions in the air. But a smooth flight never made a good pilot.

In the end, it's the learning process that makes us better people, connected to our divine creative source. All things become good, even the bad things that were meant for evil, because we have a relationship with our Creator, who is working a divine purpose in our lives. God wants to bring healing to all. He wants to give us everything we need, including a prince, if that is what we truly need to be able to fly. That is what he has done for me, and that is what he wants to do for you, as well.

Divine Love

There is nothing that will make you smarter about men than seeking to love *divinely*. Not romantic love, but *divine* love. There are three keys to the kingdom of the divine. They are *hope*, *faith*, and *love*, and the greatest of these is love.

Hope is the belief that good things are going to happen, even if things in our lives are bad now, built on the knowledge that our Creator is a good God who would never trick, manipulate, or initiate the bad things that happen to us. And it is absolutely true that if you are hopeful, you are also grateful; and if you are grateful, you will see the good things you already have.

Faith is about choosing to believe in a good Creator God, even when we cannot prove it scientifically or intellectually. It is an intuitive sense in our spirit that knows that there is something bigger than ourselves going on, and that our prayers are not in vain.

The ultimate *love* is not about romance; it is about God. Whether you are single or married, there is a prince waiting for you, inside your heart. Look to the glittering stars and think about what is waiting for you on the other side. You might find he has been there all along. And *that* is true divine love.

BONUS SECTION

And She Lived Happily Ever After...

SMART Principles for Getting Romance Right

Getting smart about men is a lot like losing weight. It is about a lifestyle change. Don't starve yourself emotionally or give up men altogether; instead, gradually begin to adopt a healthier lifestyle. You take little bitty baby steps on the path toward change.

But in case you are one of those really concrete thinkers who doesn't do well with generalizations, I've given you a five-step plan to help get you started. I've used the acronym SMART to help you remember it, with a key word or phrase central to each step.

You may not always follow the steps in the order they are

written, because change isn't always a sequential process. Usually we zigzag, sometimes we get lost on the path, and we often find ourselves right back where we started. That is natural and not a sign that you are failing. It is just a sign that you need to keep working toward your goals. After all is said and done, eventually your efforts will pay off. You will find yourself being more careful and less driven by your emotional needs and addictions.

For each step, I've offered suggestions for how to implement it. Take from those suggestions what you think will work for you; not every idea will. Each step incorporates the ten general getting romance right rules listed at the end of this chapter. The rules are the thinking processes that have to change and the five-step plan helps you integrate those new thoughts into your life and implement them on a daily basis.

Five-Step Plan for Getting Smart about Men

SUPPORT: Set goals and find *support*.

MANAGE: Learn to *manage* your thoughts and emotions.

ACTION AND ACCOUNTABILITY: Be *accountable* to others as you take *action*.

REINVENT: Begin to *reinvent* your life by introducing new behaviors.

TIME: Give yourself *time* to change and be easy on yourself in the process.

You can create your own step-by-step plan. Get a notebook and lay out a plan that works for you.

Step 1: Set Goals and Find Support

+ Begin to keep a journal of your daily thoughts, especially noting your thoughts and feelings about men, your friends, and relationships.

+ Write an encouraging letter to yourself, seal it up, and mail it to yourself to open at a future date when you feel weak and lonely.

- Ask others and God for forgiveness for past mistakes—and grant it to yourself.

- List all the good things you've got going for you apart from men.

- Create a list of positive life goals you want to achieve (career, education, weight, hobby, travel, volunteer work, etc.) without regard to time or money.

- Pick one goal that you want to achieve more than all others within the next few years and make a list of the things you would have to do to reach that goal.

- Create a rewards chart—every week give yourself a small treat (lipstick, a new book) and a nice treat (like a really nice dinner or a massage) for being smart a whole month.

- Get some of the books listed in the resource section and actually read them!

- Go to places where you are likely to meet new women who are positive influences, like professional women's clubs, church, libraries, sports events, and singles groups.

- Move slowly as you form new relationships. Don't divulge all your secrets, and work on developing relationships with older, wiser women.

- Begin researching volunteer opportunities.

- Avoid "latching on" to other women and expecting a friend to be a therapist. Consider getting counseling.

+ Give as much as you get from a friend, and get as much as you give.

+ Avoid being whiny, moody, or hypersensitive.

+ Don't adopt women in difficult situations and try to "save" them. (SAM women are notorious for this.)

+ Develop interests that attract other smart women— for example, gardening, writing, horseback riding, art, music, and travel.

+ When you get depressed and lonely, get out in public and start talking to people—deliberately smile and be helpful.

+ Say good-bye to those girls you know are bad for you.

Let me explain the last thing I've listed here: say good-bye to girls who are bad influences in your life. You've got to pay attention to the women you allow into your life, not just the men. Painful as it may be, if some girls are a big part of your problem, you've got to distance yourself until they decide they want to change, too.

If the truth is known, I'll bet a lot of your friends are just as stupid about men as you are, and you've got your own personal SAM Club going on. You go to the bars, the beach, and the ball games with each other; but the first thing you start doing when you get there is man-hunting—and that is what you talk about the rest of the week. The truth is, SAM women tend to spend their lives mainly talking about three things: the men that got away, the men they *wish* would go away, and the perfect men they hope are just around the corner.

But if you are going to change, you've got to find smart girl-friends with more going on in their lives than their obsessions with the opposite sex. Smart friends love you and stick with you even when it isn't required—even when they are mad at you, neglect you on occasion, or disappear every now and then. Deep down you know they are there at the end of the day, and if something goes terribly wrong in your life, they will be the first to hop on the plane to get to your side. A good friend will encourage you, support you, and believe in your ability to change, and will not be afraid to get in your face every now and then to smack some sense into you. If you already have a friend like that, hang on to her for dear life!

Step 2: Manage *Your* Thoughts

+ Start every day with a prayer asking God to help you.

+ Read a devotion, an inspirational book, and sing a song that inspires you.

+ Begin to eliminate music, television programs, novels, movies, and newspapers that encourage romantic addiction.

+ Interrupt negative thoughts when they occur by saying "STOP IT" out loud.

+ Wear a bracelet or a piece of jewelry that reminds you to avoid negative thinking.

+ Avoid conversations with coworkers who gossip or make fun of you.

+ Begin to eliminate words from your language that are part of your old identity (like curse words, crude language, graphic references to sex, etc.).

+ Avoid talking about men with other women.

+ Control your fantasy life.

+ In your journal, begin to identify circumstances that seem to trigger old behaviors.

+ Once you identify the triggers, chart how often they happen on a daily basis. Look for recurring patterns. If you do not see a decline, get counseling to help you.

+ Every day spend some quiet time visualizing yourself being happy, successful, and strong.

Controlling your thought life is really about self-discipline. But disciplining your thoughts is not the same as wrestling with them. Sometimes the more we wrestle, the more we get taken down on the mat. Think of your thoughts as unruly children and you as the parent. It is not a power struggle to see who will win out; rather, take authority over the situation.

That leads to the next step:

Step 3: *Take* Action *and Be* Accountable

+ Find one good friend who will understand what you are doing and allow her to assess your progress on a weekly basis.

- Add three things back into your life that you used to enjoy doing as a child, like horseback riding, playing an instrument, or getting a puppy.

- Enroll in one class that increases your skills and knowledge base at work or makes you feel more competent in your life (like cooking, Web design, etc.).

- Join a church or a support group of your choice.

- Open a savings account and start saving money.

- Plan a little vacation to somewhere you want to go, even if that means going alone (which could be quite therapeutic!).

- Pick a volunteer opportunity and sign up to work at least an hour once a week.

- If you are in an unhealthy relationship, get counseling.

- If you are married or in a relationship that is abusive and counseling is not an option, make a list of all the things that would need to happen for you to be able to leave peacefully.

- Try to eat healthier and begin to exercise. Make a promise to take care of yourself.

- Begin to eliminate items of clothing in your wardrobe that are too big, too tight, too short, or too revealing.

- Permanently end any unhealthy relationship if you possibly can.

- Stop enabling an alcoholic or drug user, and stop allowing a man to use you to pay the bills. Show him the door.

+ If you have children and they are having problems, get counseling for them.

+ Get professional help for depression, anxiety, etc. if you cannot get a handle on your emotions.

Step 4: Reinvent *Yourself*

+ Write an essay describing what you want your life to look like five years from now. Read it once a week. Be as specific and detailed as possible.

+ Volunteer for a major mission trip out of the country or plan a significant spiritual journey of some kind (like visiting Israel, Rome, or your family's place of origin).

+ Make a donation to a charity, whatever you can afford.

+ If you have tattoos that bring back painful memories, get them removed. Conversely, if you feel you've turned a new leaf and want to memorialize it, perhaps get a tattoo!

+ If you have provocative profiles on places like MySpace. com, dismantle them or replace them with more positive images that are not focused on attracting men and romance.

+ Begin to work on your college degree or the next credential you need for success.

+ You may need to move to a new apartment or a new town and get a fresh start.

+ You may need to get a job that is more challenging and allows more growth instead of a job that just pays the bills while you are bored to death.

Step 5: Give Yourself Time

+ Allow yourself *at least* a year for your thinking to truly change.

+ When you stumble, find people who will support you and share your mistakes.

+ Seek short-term counseling to get back on track.

+ Read that letter of encouragement you wrote to yourself in step 1.

+ Forgive yourself and start over.

The Ten Rules
for
Getting Romance Right

RULE 1
Choose a good man, not a financial plan.

RULE 2
Decide to be happy now;
don't wait for someone to make you happy.

RULE 3
Know that it is more important to be smart than sexy.

RULE 4
Care for yourself as much as you care for your man.

RULE 5
Don't waste your time trying to be perfect.

RULE 6
Whenever possible, tell the truth.

RULE 7
Change yourself, not your man.

RULE 8
Steer clear of the bad boys.

RULE 9
Choose the right man,
not just the first one who comes along.

RULE 10
Find your soul, then someone
who brings out the best in you.

The SAM Syndrome:

When Being Stupid Gets Really Serious

There is no doubt that the majority of women who read this book do *not* have a problem with men so severe that it could almost be defined as a "syndrome." But this section is for women who do, and is designed to help you decide if you might need professional help in your attempts to grow smart about men.

Primarily, the SAM syndrome comes from *cognitive distortions*, a term therapists use to describe the flawed thinking and ideas about how reality and relationships are supposed to work. And those flaws, like viewing oneself in a fun house mirror, give the viewer a distorted perception of life. They are often accompanied by negative thinking, behavior disorders, risky behaviors, extremes in emotion, impulsivity, promiscuity, sequential marriage and divorce, or a series of long-term relationships that do not end in commitment.

The following is a brief overview of thought distortions and the behaviors that result. If many items on this list describe you and a pattern of failed relationships seems to be emerging in your life, this could mean that you need further help.

How a Woman with the SAM Syndrome Thinks

+ My value as a woman is determined by a man.

+ My self-image is in direct proportion to my sexual desirability.

+ Divine love and romantic love are the same.

+ The purpose of life is to find true love.

+ If a man does not love me, God has forgotten me.

+ If a man is not in love with me, something is wrong with me.

+ Sexual intimacy will cause a man to fall in love with me.

+ I must find the perfect man.

+ If I cannot find a perfect man, I can change the man I find.

+ The power of my love can change a man.

+ To be needed is to be loved.

+ It is a man's job to take care of me.

+ I cannot take care of myself.

+ If I am lonely, then I must not be loved.

+ If a man loves me, he will be obsessed with me.

+ Jealousy is a sign of true love.

+ Truth is whatever I want it to be.

+ If I want something badly enough, I will get it.

+ If I pretend something is true, it will become true.

+ I will magically achieve a happy life.

How a Woman with the SAM Syndrome Behaves

+ Constantly compares herself to other women.

+ Is self-critical and obsessed with weight, appearance, and clothing.

+ Complains frequently of loneliness and a fear that life is passing her by.

+ Is impulsive in love and enters into sexual intimacy too soon.

+ May detach and reattach to men very quickly.

+ Continually talks about failed romantic relationships.

+ Won't listen to anyone else when she is in love.

+ Continually makes excuses for and protects the man she loves.

+ Obsesses about relationship failures or her ability to "find a man."

+ May overlook good men because they aren't sexy or rich.

+ Often suffers from depression or other mood disorders.

+ Does not seem to learn from past mistakes.

+ Is drawn to emotionally unstable men she must rescue.

+ Is drawn to men who will rescue her.

+ Has a high degree of need for excitement and intensity in relationships.

+ Is caught in a cycle of repeating patterns with inappropriate partners.

+ Tends to sabotage good relationships for no apparent reason.

+ Uses romance as a form of addictive behavior.

+ May cycle in and out of the same bad relationship with one man.

+ Has a dramatic romantic life, with many highs and lows.

+ Is often attracted to emotionally unavailable, married, or dangerous men.

+ Has a history of abuse in the past and continues to allow men to abuse her in the present.

Discussion Group Guide

1. Fantasies about the fairy-tale life abound in our culture. Share the expectations you have of romance and men. Are those expectations realistic or unrealistic? Why?

2. Discuss times when you've employed magical thinking in your life.

3. The author, Deborah, states that women cannot change men. Do you think there are exceptions? If you've seen an exception to the rule, discuss the nature of the change and what made these situations different from the norm. How difficult was the process?

4. It's clear that mothering men is not healthy behavior. However, we live in a culture where women are pressured to take care of others, often at the expense of their own well-being. Discuss when it is appropriate to take care of others, how some women confuse being needed with being loved, and ways women can restore a healthy balance in their relationships.

5. Women experience a great deal of pressure to "be perfect." Discuss how this has impacted your own relationships with men.

6. The story of Snow White is used as a metaphor for depression and sleeping one's life away. Identify an opportunity you may have missed in life because you distracted yourself in an unhealthy manner or were too afraid to take a chance. Discuss what you may be able to do to turn a new leaf and accomplish those goals you once missed.

7. Loneliness can be crushing at times, but it can be manageable. Share times in your life when you successfully managed loneliness.

8. Discuss the ways women sometimes settle for second best in their lives and how to know when they are acting out of fear, or when they are actually making a wise choice.

9. Discuss the difference between sexual intimacy and emotional intimacy. Perhaps even share personal experiences that help you clarify the difference in your own mind.

10. If appropriate for your group, share what you learned from your parents that might influence the way you behave in romantic relationships.

11. How can "denial" become a defense mechanism to avoid accepting truth?

12. What predisposes women to become attracted to dangerous or emotionally troubled men?

13. Review the SMART principles and discuss which elements of the list may be helpful for each member of your group. If you're feeling particularly motivated, make a step-by-step action plan based on the principles and support one another in the growth process.

Notes

Chapter 3: Tinker Bell

1. *Healthy Youth!* National Center for Chronic Disease Prevention and Health Promotion, www.cdc.gov/HealthyYouth.

2. *Facts on Induced Abortion in the United States,* New York: Guttmacher Institute, January 2008.

3. Ali, Lorraine, and Lisa Miller, "The Secret Lives of Wives," *Newsweek,* July 12, 2004.

4. U.S. Census Bureau, *"Current Population Reports,"* Statistical Abstract of the United States, Washington, D.C.: Government Printing Office, 2008.

5. DivorceMagazine.com, U.S. Divorce Statistics, www.divorce mag.com/statistics/statsUS.shtml.

6. Laura Sessions Stepp, "Study Says Romance Makes for Safer Sex," *Washington Post,* March 4, 2008.

7. "CDC HIV/AIDS Fact Sheet," Atlanta, Ga.: Centers for Disease Control and Prevention, June 2007.

Resource List

GOOD BOOKS FOR GETTING SMARTER

Bass, Ellen, and Laura Davis. *The Courage to Heal: A Guide for Women Survivors of Child Sexual Abuse; 20th Anniversary Edition.* New York, NY: HarperCollins, 2008.

Beattie, Melody. *Codependent No More.* Center City, MN: Hazelton Foundation, 1987.

Bernstein, Albert J. *Emotional Vampires: Dealing with the People Who Drain You Dry.* New York, NY: McGraw-Hill, 2001.

Bernstein, Jeffrey, PhD, and Susan Magee. *Why Can't You Read My Mind?: Overcoming the 9 Toxic Thought Patterns that Get in the Way of a Loving Relationship.* New York, NY: Da Capo Press, 2003.

Bradshaw, John. *Reclaiming Virtue: How We Can Develop the Moral Intelligence to Do the Right Thing at the Right Time, for the Right Reason.* New York, NY: Bantam, forthcoming.

Carder, Dave, et al. *Secrets of Your Family Tree: Healing for Adult Children of Dysfunctional Families*. Chicago, IL: Moody Press, 1991.

Cloninger, Claire, and Karla Worley. *When the Glass Slipper Doesn't Fit*. Birmingham, AL: New Hope Publishers, 2000.

Cox, Michelle, and John Perrodin, eds. *Simple Little Words: What You Say Can Change a Life*. Colorado Springs, CO: Honor Books, 2008.

Elliot, Elisabeth. *Passion and Purity: Learning to Bring Your Love Life under Christ's Control*. Grand Rapids, MI: Revell, 2002.

———. *The Path of Loneliness: Finding Your Way through the Wilderness to God*. Grand Rapids, MI: Revell, 2007.

Everson, Eva Marie, and Jessica Everson. *Sex, Lies, and the Media*. Colorado Springs, CO: Life Journey, 2005.

Farrel, Bill and Pam. *Men Are Like Waffles, Women Are Like Spaghetti*. Eugene, OR: Harvest House Publishers, 2001.

Freitas, Donna. *Sex and the Soul: Juggling Sexuality, Spirituality, Romance, and Religion on America's College Campuses*. New York, NY: Oxford University Press, 2008.

Gardner, James, MD, and Arthur H. Bell, PhD. *Overcoming Anxiety, Panic, and Depression: New Ways to Regain your Confidence*. Franklin Lakes, NJ: Career Press, 2000.

Glass, Shirley P., PhD, with Jean Coppock Staeheli. *Not "Just Friends": Rebuilding Trust and Recovering Your Sanity After Infidelity*. New York: NY, Free Press, 2004.

Goleman, Daniel. *Emotional Intelligence: Why It Can Matter More Than IQ*. New York, NY: Bantam, 2005.

Halpern, Howard M., PhD. *How to Break Your Addiction to a Person*. New York, NY: Bantam, 2004.

Hart, Archibald, PhD, and Catherine Hart Weber, PhD. *A Woman's Guide to Overcoming Depression*. Grand Rapids, MI: Revell, 2007.

Hendrix, Harville. *Getting the Love You Want: A Guide for Couples*. New York, NY: Owl Books, 2001.

Hendrix, Harville, and Helen Lakelly Hunt. *Receiving Love: Transform Your Relationship by Letting Yourself Be Loved*. New York, NY: Atria, 2004.

Henry, Patti: *The Emotionally Unavailable Man: A Blueprint for Healing*. Highland City, FL: Rainbow Books, 2004.

Hotchkiss, Sandy, LCSW. *Why Is It Always About You?: The Seven Deadly Sins of Narcissism*. New York, NY: Free Press, 2003.

Kiley, Dan. *The Peter Pan Syndrome: Men Who Have Never Grown Up*. New York, NY: Avon, 1995.

Lamott, Anne. *Traveling Mercies: Some Thoughts on Faith*. New York, NY: Random House, 1999.

Leaf, Caroline, Dr. *Who Switched Off My Brain?: Controlling Toxic Thoughts and Emotions*. Dallas, TX: Switch On Your Brain USA, 2007.

Love, Pat, EdD. *The Truth About Love: The Highs, the Lows, and How You Can Make It Last Forever.* New York, NY: Fireside, 2001.

McManus, Mike and Harriet. *Living Together: Myths, Risks, & Answers.* New York, NY: Howard Books, 2008.

Meyer, Joyce. *Approval Addiction: Overcoming Your Need to Please Everyone.* New York, NY: Warner Faith, 2005.

Moore, Beth. *Get Out of That Pit: Straight Talk about God's Deliverance.* Nashville, TN: Integrity Publishers, 2007.

Murphy, Tim, and Loriann Hoff Oberlin. *Overcoming Passive-Aggression: How to Stop Hidden Anger from Spoiling Your Relationships, Career and Happiness.* New York, NY: Marlowe & Company, 2005.

Norwood, Robin. *Women Who Love Too Much.* New York, NY: Simon & Schuster, 1990.

Peabody, Susan. *Addiction to Love: Overcoming Obsession and Dependency in Relationships.* Berkeley, CA: Celestial Arts, 2005.

Petherbridge, Laura. *When "I Do" Becomes "I Don't."* Colorado Springs, CO: David C. Cook, 2008.

Phillips, Bob. *Overcoming Anxiety and Depression.* Eugene, OR: Harvest House Publishers, 2007.

Schlessinger, Laura. *Bad Childhood—Good Life: How to Blossom and Thrive in Spite of an Unhappy Childhood.* New York, NY: HarperCollins, 2006.

Simon, George K., Jr., PhD. *In Sheep's Clothing: Understanding and Dealing with Manipulative People*. Little Rock, AR: A. J. Christopher, 1996.

Smalley, Gary, et al. *The DNA of Relationships*. Wheaton, IL: Tyndale House Publishers, 2004.

Spring, Janus Abrahams, PhD. *How Can I Forgive You?: The Courage to Forgive, the Freedom Not To*. New York, NY: HarperCollins, 2004.

Van Epp, John. *How to Avoid Marrying a Jerk: The Foolproof Way to Follow Your Heart Without Losing Your Mind*. New York, NY: McGraw-Hill, 2007.

Vernick, Leslie. *The Emotionally Destructive Relationship: Seeing It, Stopping It, Surviving It*. Eugene, OR: Harvest House Publishers, 2007.

Whelan, Christine B. *Why Smart Men Marry Smart Women*. New York, NY: Simon & Schuster, 2006.

Wright, H. Norman. *Communication: Key to Your Marriage; A Practical Guide to Creating a Happy, Fulfilling Relationship*. Ventura, CA: Regal Books, 2000.

WEBSITES

Alcoholics Anonymous
www.aa.org

Adult Survivors of Child Abuse
www.ascasupport.org

ConsumerAffairs.com
www.consumeraffairs.com

National Mental Health Information Center
www.mentalhealth.samhsa.gov

Marriage Savers
www.marriagesavers.org

National Eating Disorders Association (NEDA)
www.nationaleatingdisorders.org

National Association for Anorexia Nervosa and
Associated Eating Disorders (ANAD)
www.anad.org

Romance Scam
www.romancescam.com

SCAMwatch
www.scamwatch.gov.au

American Foundation for Healing
for Survivors of Sexual Abuse
www.stopsexualabusenow.org

Sassy Pink Peppers—
support group for divorced women
www.sassypinkpeppers.com

The National Domestic Violence Hotline
www.ndvh.org
1-800-799-SAFE

Christianity.com
www.christianity.com

God Tube
www.godtube.com

Shout Life—Christian social community
www.shoutlife.com

Crosswalk.com
www.crosswalk.com

Check www.stupidaboutmen.com for links to more websites.

About the Author

Deborah Dunn is a licensed marriage and family therapist in private practice near Raleigh, North Carolina. She specializes in helping people recover from crises and move forward with their lives by focusing on positive, life-affirming goals and emotional and spiritual health. Her career spans twenty years and includes such diverse experience as working as an intensive family preservation specialist and as a foster care social worker, with abused and neglected children, for the state of North Carolina. She also works with her husband as a residential teaching parent in a group home for children and at one point worked extensively with victims of violence as the manager of a shelter for battered women. It is in those roles that she developed a passion for helping women rise above lifelong patterns of poor choices in romance and start the journey toward being smarter about men and about life in general.

She is also the founder of Community Crisis, Inc., a nonprofit disaster-education organization that teaches community disaster resilience and disaster planning in small, economically distressed rural areas. In addition, she has developed a program, Called to Crisis, that provides corporate crisis intervention services after such events as bank robberies, on-site employee deaths, suicides, and corporate downsizing.

Deborah travels and speaks all over the United States, sharing her life-changing message of resiliency, hope, and positive transformation. She and her husband, Rick, live near Raleigh, North Carolina, and have two adult children and a beautiful granddaughter. Deborah loves to sculpt, paint, and garden when her busy schedule allows. You can learn more about her and join her online social community at www.deborahdunn.com.